The Kickstarter Companion

Answers to Questions You Didn't Know You Had

Heidi Berthiaume

Kickstarter Companion

Published by Bengal Studio
PO Box 863926
Plano, TX 75086

Printed in the USA

www.kscompanion.com

Dedication

For my mom and dad,
lifelong supporters of my projects

Acknowledgments

Writing a book is a solitary activity but getting a book refined and out to an audience takes a village. I'm fortunate to have some very fine folks in my village …

The backers of my 1000 Origami Wish Cranes Kickstarter project who proved a Kickstarter project can be whatever you want it to be …

The creators who have hired me to manage their Kickstarter projects, because while I helped them, their questions and insights helped me better know what information to put into this book …

The backers of my *Kickstarter Companion* Kickstarter project who helped fund the production of what you now hold in your hands …

My beta readers who let me know how to better this book: Vicky, J.T., Karen, and Melissa …

Joshua Essoe for editing and Jeremy Owen for design and layout help …

Kevin J. Anderson for the hug, the conversation, and the free book …

James A. Owen for advice, trust, writing the Foreword, and the first-hand experience of what it takes to fulfill an 800+ backer Kickstarter project …

And J.T. Entzminger for all kinds of support, including listening, food delivery, encouragement, and quite a few Starbucks chai tea lattes.

My deepest gratitude and appreciation for everyone's time and effort on my behalf.

Table Of Contents

How To Get Unstuck:
A Foreword from the Periphery

In a world of increasing specialization, there are many opportunities available to those who are willing and able to make a livelihood out of advising, counseling, and consulting. There are few things as gratifying as finding yourself stuck (literally and/or figuratively) in any kind of endeavor, then suddenly having an expert in whatever it is that you were doing suddenly appear and explain to you how to become unstuck, so that you can continue to move forward in pursuit of your goals.

One of my all-time favorite movies is TUCKER: A MAN AND HIS DREAM, about the entrepreneur, inventor, enthusiast, and all-around eccentric Preston Tucker. Post World War II, he made a car that was so advanced, so stylish, and so apparently superior to every other existing vehicle that the Big Automakers had to rally political and legal support to try to shut him down before people realized just how awesome his car, the Tucker Torpedo, really was. They succeeded—but not before he built fifty of the most remarkable cars ever made.

In the film, a young engineer, fresh from college and about to exit the military showed up at Tucker's door and politely requested five minutes of the inventor's time. Tucker was distracted, but agreed to hear the kid out. The young man pulled out some drawings of the Tucker Torpedo he had done based on pictures of the car and an interview Tucker had given that had been published in a magazine. The thing was, the drawings were different than Tucker's designs;

the kid had changed several aspects of the car, including key features that Tucker considered all but sacred.

The inventor asked the engineer why he would change the designs, and the kid answered, "Because, sir, the way you designed it just won't work. But with my changes, it'll still be the same beautiful car you designed, it'll just work better."

Still distracted, Tucker turned to go into the house, and the kid pleaded with him to just consider his suggestions. "What do you want?" Tucker asked. "A job? You've got it."

Flabbergasted, the kid stammered "In the Design Department?"

Tucker smiled his famous smile and replied, "Kid, you ARE the Design Department."

Heidi Berthiaume is my Design Department.

I wrote a book, DRAWING OUT THE DRAGONS: A Meditation on Art, Destiny, and the Power Of Choice, that Heidi read, absorbed, and decided she wanted to know more about. So she connected with me online, watched, took notes, and then essentially showed up at my door with suggestions on how I could do everything I was doing BETTER. She offered advice that was grounded in common sense, and careful observation, and did not change the books I had written, but helped their message to come across more clearly. Her counsel has helped my business to run more smoothly and efficiently, and she has given me no less than her absolute support in everything I have undertaken to do.

Much of what made her consults so valuable was that she had found answers to questions I didn't know I had. And when I had questions she hadn't yet considered, she found the answers to those, too.

The greatest compliment I ever heard someone give was at the funeral of one of my closest friends, a man named James Chapple. His brother spoke about how James was always trying to learn about the things the people around him did and loved, so that he could help them do those things better. "It sometimes seemed," his brother said, "that James was more committed to achieving your goals than YOU were."

It sometimes seems that way with Heidi Berthiaume, too. She is one of the principal reasons my first Kickstarter, to do a print edition of DRAWING OUT THE DRAGONS, succeeded. She was a prime mover in the success of my second Kickstarter for a hardcover collection of the STARCHILD comic book series I created years ago. And true to form, she didn't just learn by observing, but also by actively participating, when she created her own Kickstarter to produce 1000 Origami Wish Cranes (like the one featured on the cover of this book), which succeeded spectacularly well, and which also gave her many valuable insights into how Kickstarter works.

Those insights and more are what she shares in this book. The subtitle, "Answers to Questions You Didn't Know You Had" is an apt one. That's where the value lies in this book: not in the things you already know, but in the things you might not have expected, that have caused you to become stuck in one way or another. Heidi Berthiaume can help you become unstuck, because she's done her homework. She IS the Design Department you need. And she is committed to helping you to reach your goals.

The information in this book probably won't change the nature of WHAT you are doing with your Kickstarter project; but it will make everything about DOING your Kickstarter project BETTER than you would do without it. I don't think I can offer a higher recommendation than that.

James A. Owen
Silvertown, Arizona
March 4, 2014

Introduction

"Creativity is contagious, pass it on."– Albert Einstein

It takes a lot of courage to share your idea with the world. It takes even more courage to ask the world for money to make your idea a reality.

Kickstarter lets you do both. If you are willing to do the work necessary, you can use Kickstarter to raise money to turn your idea into something real. People pledge toward your project's funding goal and if your funding goal is achieved, you send those people rewards based on the amount of money they pledged.

Kickstarter is crowdfunding for projects that result in the creation of some thing. It can be a book, a film, a CD, art prints, a photography exhibit, clothing, a video game, a drinking carafe, a theater production, or salsa. A project can be as big as making a movie based on a canceled television series or as small as buying paper to fold origami Wish Cranes.

Your project can ask for thousands of dollars or only $25, it doesn't matter. What does matter is that you provide something in return to the people who give you their money.

Kickstarter is not charity—if you don't meet your funding goal, you don't get any money from your backers. They, in turn, don't get any of the rewards of your project, so it's in everyone's best interest to have a successful project.

Each project on Kickstarter is unique, because every creator has a different vision of how to realize their idea. A creator also has to present their project in accordance with the information required by the Kickstarter website, such as:

- A project image
- A written description
- A pledge level (a monetary amount and a description)
- Rewards (items sent to backers)
- A funding goal (amount of money to be raised)
- A duration (amount of time the campaign will run)
- Text regarding risks and challenges

The folks at Kickstarter highly recommended you have a video, saying "Projects with videos succeed at a much higher rate than those without (50% vs. 30%)." However, having a video isn't necessary to get your project launched.

The Kickstarter website has several pages of information about how to run a project. Even though I'd read those website pages before I ran my "1000 Origami Wish Cranes" project (http://www.kickstarter.com/projects/heidi2524/1000-origami-wish-cranes) in the summer of 2013, I still ended up with a lot questions. That's why I wanted to write this book—to answer those questions in detail with recommendations based on running my own successful Kickstarter project, managing other successful projects, backing over eighty projects, and reviewing hundreds more.

Who This Book Can Help

The information in here can help the following kinds of folks:

- Those who have never run a Kickstarter project
- Those who have run a Kickstarter project
- Those who have run a bunch of Kickstarter projects

For those who have never run a Kickstarter project, I recommend reading the information on the Kickstarter website. Look through the Start page (http://www.kickstarter.com/learn) and the Our Rules page (http://www.kickstarter.com/rules). That will get you through the basics of what's going on and give you a framework to think about your project. The information in this book will help you get through the details of defining your project, creating your project Home page, running your campaign, and then fulfilling your promises by delivering the rewards to your backers.

For those who have a Kickstarter project under your belt, you already know more than the basics. The information about defining pledge levels, creating a timeline, or recommendations for the project description could be useful for your next project.

For those who have run a bunch of Kickstarter projects, you probably get a lot of questions from people about how to create a successful project. In that case, this book is an excellent resource you can share with those folks to get them up to speed before talking to them about the specifics of their project.

Why I Wrote This Book

I've been a backer on Kickstarter since 2009 when a friend sent me a link to fund his independent film. Once on the site, I was amazed at the variety of projects. So many unique ideas and different funding goals. I saw things on Kickstarter that I knew I'd never see in a store. But there, on that website, I could help those people realize their ideas and in return for my money, get a copy of that board game, or bracelet, or DVD of a play. And often some nice additional swag, depending at what level I pledged.

Over the years, I've backed more than eighty Kickstarter projects and looked at hundreds more. Some funded, some didn't. Some relaunched their project and funded on the second try. With a career background in information architecture and communication, and an attention to detail that can't be turned off, I ended up analyzing any project I looked at to find out what works, what doesn't, and what could be done better.

I talk a lot about Kickstarter and promote the projects I support, so people who know me know I love Kickstarter. When some of those people decided to run their own Kickstarter projects, they asked for my help. While I could advise them from a backer's perspective, I didn't have the experience to speak from a creator's perspective.

I decided to run my own Kickstarter project to better understand what it takes to craft a project from beginning to end, from idea to shipping.

The "1000 Origami Wish Cranes" project was a valuable experience because creating a project meant I had to come up with all of the information that backers take for granted: text, video, pledge levels, and graphics. It took some work, and time, and while Kickstarter had good information on their website to walk me through the process at a high level, I ended up with a lot of unanswered questions.

My Wish Cranes project ran for 30 days in the summer of 2013. It over-funded by 6,180%. I didn't do that math by the way; the Kickstarter Dashboard did it for me.

Part of that over-funding was because I had the two-digit funding goal of $25 and ended up with over 270 backers. Part of that over-funding was because I did the things I think make a Kickstarter project more likely to succeed.

That summer, I also managed a Kickstarter project for a friend that ended up over-funding by 328%. I don't take credit for the project being a success as he had an established audience who wanted those rewards. I will take credit for the video, the pledge graphics, and the editing of the pledge levels, including reducing one pledge level description from 41 lines to seven.

So a lot more folks ask me about Kickstarter these days.

And I found a lot of them had the same questions—how to structure their pledge levels, what to put in the video, how to come up with the funding goal, etc. Some I work with as clients and manage their Kickstarter projects. My time is limited, though, so I can't work directly with everyone.

What I can do is write up the answers to the common questions, provide details about how to more efficiently work with the Kickstarter website, and point out things to consider and think about before, during, and after you run your campaign.

Other than a few commonalities that are required by Kickstarter, every project is unique. I can't tell if a project will fund or not (because I've seen some amazing last minute saves), but I believe there are specific things creators can do to best assure their projects have a fighting chance.

That's why I wrote this book.

And that's why there's an origami Wish Crane on the cover.

What's In This Book

The Kickstarter website has a lot of good information to help you create your project. This book has a lot of detailed information to answer questions you may have while creating your project, as well as questions you didn't know you had until you tried.

In order to cover everything I want to cover, I've created the following sections:

A Bit About Kickstarter

First, there is a quick introduction to three important things you need to understand about Kickstarter. I also cover what kind of equipment is required to run a project.

Factors Of A Successful Project

I believe there are three factors to a successful Kickstarter project and all of them are within your control. There are also a few pages on the Kickstarter website that can help you with promoting your project.

Before You Start

You have to sign up for a Kickstarter account and I highly recommend you back at least one project before creating your own. You can also use websites such as Kicktraq and Kickspy to study what happens to a Kickstarter project during its campaign.

Anatomy Of A Kickstarter Project

This section covers the common elements and how information displays on the project Home page. There's also a breakdown of the Updates page, the Backers page, and the Comments page.

Part 1: Define Your Project

Here I'll walk you through several steps to help you define your project. First, you'll need to pick a category and sub-category. Second is the funding goal, which is reached by figuring out your project expenses, rewards' costs, packaging, shipping, fees, and taxes. Then you can define your pledge levels. Now is also a good time to give some thoughts to stretch goals and whether or not you want to have any add-ons (also sometimes known as a la carte items). I'll also go through how to create a timeline with important dates for project pre-launch, the duration of the campaign, and fulfillment.

Part 2: Create Your Project

I'll review how to set up your project using each of the Project Tabs on the Kickstarter website. When you're ready, you can create a Preview of your project Home page for feedback, then try the Launch Now feature or submit your project for review by a Kickstarter Community Manager.

Part 3: Run Your Campaign

Once your project is live, you'll use the Creator Tools to manage your project and maintain your project Home page. I've included some more promotion ideas in this section as well as how to communicate with your backers via updates, comments, and messages.

Part 4: Fulfill Your Promises

After your project has successfully funded, you'll receive the money and need to get the rewards made. It's also important to keep in touch with your backers. I'll cover sending the backer surveys, how to use the information in your backer report spreadsheets, and some last comments on shipping.

What If Your Project Doesn't Fund?

If your project doesn't fund, I have a few thoughts on what you could do next.

What's Not In This Book

There are two things you won't find in my book and I want to let you know why:

- Absolute must-do/must-not-do lists
- Success stories

Absolute Must-Do/Must-Not-Do Lists

Other than the information required by Kickstarter, you won't find lists of "things you must do" or "things you should never do" in my book.

I don't believe in those kinds of absolutes for Kickstarter projects. What works awesomely for one project may not work for another because each project truly is unique. When I have a recommendation, I'll let you know. If it sounds like something that would benefit your project, do it. If not, don't.

A lot of advice is available on how to run a successful Kickstarter project. The Kickstarter website has links in the footer to a searchable FAQ, the Creator Handbook, and a blog where they announce updates they've made to the site and project process. Read articles online, talk to people, think about what you've read and what's been said, and then decide what *you* want to do.

Success Stories

Because each Kickstarter project is unique, from what shows on the project Home page to how the creators run their campaign to who they are and their connections to other people, I don't have any success stories in this book. There are too many categories of projects to put in enough success stories that would be meaningful for every reader. The story of a thousands-of-dollars-over-funded video game won't necessarily help someone trying to fund the creation of a CD.

If you want to learn how a project was successful, read creator interviews and success stories as much as you want ... and then study a successful project. Especially a successful project that's similar to what you want to do.

There's more information on how to look up the history of a project on the Kicktraq and Kickspy websites as well as things to consider when studying a project (successful or not) in the "Before You Start" section.

Reviewing other projects will give you more information and details than what usually shows up in the typical success story write-up. And because you get to pick which successful project to study, what you learn will be more meaningful to your own project than any success story I could provide.

A Bit About Kickstarter

Started in 2009, Kickstarter is one of several online venues where you can create a webpage to ask people for money to fund a project or cause. Kickstarter is project-based, while other websites focus on raising money for charities or personal causes such as paying medical bills or in memorial of someone.

This means of raising money is often called "crowdfunding" or "crowdsourcing." The funding goal is reached by many people contributing small amounts. This is the opposite of angel investors, or venture capitalists, or the traditional patron model in which one person or a few people provide the money to have something created.

The great thing about Kickstarter is it can work for a project of any size. Millions of dollars have been raised on Kickstarter as well as just $25. The big projects get a lot of press, but your project can be for any funding amount. Most successful projects fund for under $10,000. About 44% of the projects launched on the Kickstarter website successfully reach their goal. You can see the current statistics for all projects that have ever launched on the Kickstarter Stats page (http://www.kickstarter.com/help/stats).

An important part of the Kickstarter model is while you have to pay them a fee if your project successfully funds, you keep 100% ownership of your project. Same thing goes for backers—even though they're pledging money to your project, you're compensating them with rewards, not ownership or any kind of claim on your intellectual property.

You also need to understand that when you launch a project, it'll be on the Kickstarter website as long as there is a Kickstarter website. Whether or not your project funds, it'll still be on the Kickstarter website and can be found via their search function. Canceled and suspended projects also remain on the Kickstarter website. And even if you delete your account, yes, your project will still show up on the Kickstarter website.

Three Important Things

I believe there are three important things to understand about using Kickstarter:

- You must fund a project
- Your project must fit into a category
- Kickstarter is an all-or-nothing funding model

You Must Fund A Project

Kickstarter defines a project as "something with a clear end, like making an album, a film, or a new game. A project will eventually be completed, and something will be produced as a result."

The things "produced as a result" are delivered to your backers as rewards for pledging money to help you complete your project. The rewards can be electronic (a PDF of a comic or novel, an MP3 of a song or an entire album) or tangible (printed book, CD, DVD), or a combination of both—whatever is appropriate for your project.

For my Wish Cranes project, the "clear end" was that I folded one thousand origami cranes. Depending on their pledge level, backers were mailed one to seven of the paper cranes.

You can raise money for just about anything with Kickstarter as long as it is a project that produces rewards for your backers.

Your Project Must Fit Into A Category

Kickstarter has a list of predetermined categories including Art, Dance, Fashion, Film & Video, Food, Music, Publishing, Technology, etc. All categories also have sub-categories, such as Animation or Documentary under Film & Video.

Picking a category helps your potential backers understand your project at a high level. With that out of the way, your project Home page can get into the details of what makes your project unique within that category.

Kickstarter Is An All-Or-Nothing Funding Model

If your project doesn't reach its funding goal by the end of the campaign, no money will be taken from backers. If you make your funding goal, you get the money. If you don't, you won't.

Other crowdfunding websites, such as IndieGoGo, allow a project to choose a funding model: all-or-nothing or "flexible funding." Flexible funding means all of the money raised, even if it's less than the funding goal, will be collected from backers and delivered to the creator of the project.

A NOTE ABOUT CONTENT AND COPYRIGHT: All of the content you use on your project Home page must have been created by you or licensed for use. This includes the text, images, video, audio, music, and sound effects. You can't show a video clip from a Hollywood movie nor use a band's song without their permission. There are several places online to get royalty-free images, audio, and video, and other places where you can pay a fee to license such things.

For my Wish Cranes project, I created all of the images and the video using my own photography. I licensed the music used in the video from Stereobot (http://www.stereobot.com).

For the Kickstarter project that funded the editing, ebook formatting, and printing of the limited edition copies of this book, I again created all of the images and video using my own photography. The music in the video was licensed from Pond5 (http://www.pond5.com).

What You Need

Because Kickstarter is a website, you need access to a computer that has an Internet connection and a web browser such as Internet Explorer, Firefox, Chrome, or Safari.

I specifically say "computer" compared to tablet or smartphone, because it's going to be easier to create all the content (text, images, video, etc.) you need for your project Home page as well as deal with the backer information

Kickstarter provides in the form of spreadsheets on a laptop or desktop. You can use any kind of computer that can access the Kickstarter website since your project is set up entirely online.

You're also going to need some time, a bit of patience, and an idea.

You don't need any money to put your project on the Kickstarter website, that part is completely free.

Most creators have already spent some money on their projects, or are partially funded and ask backers for the money needed to complete the project. At the very least, you need to create enough content to explain your idea on your project Home page so people understand what your project is and what they'll receive as their rewards.

One Last Thing

Kickstarter has a very active community and as a company, is continually working on improving the experience of the creators and backers who use the website. This means some of the information in this book will get out of sync as the website gets updated.

Just in the months it took to write this book and run the Kickstarter project that funded it, several website enhancements happened. The basics of what a project is and how to create one remained the same, but some of the details changed, often for the better. I've done the best I can to make this book as accurate as possible as of mid-June 2014.

Factors Of A Successful Project

As mentioned earlier, I don't have any absolutes that will make a Kickstarter project successful. I do believe there are three distinct factors that have a direct effect on whether or not a funding goal is reached:

- What your project is
- How you set up your project
- How your promote your project

What Your Project Is

Your Kickstarter project is determined by you. It's your idea, your decision to use Kickstarter, your effort that makes it possible for other people to see what you're doing and maybe help fund it.

Your project will either connect with enough people to fund or it won't.

How You Set Up Your Project

The only information a potential backer knows about your idea and what you're trying to accomplish is what you put on your project Home page. If they have a question, they may contact you, but that requires effort on their part. It's easier to find a different project to support that doesn't leave them with unanswered questions.

Therefore how you set up your project, from the funding goal to the text and images in the project description to the structure of the pledge levels, is incredibly important—and completely up to you.

How You Promote Your Project

Ideally, the more people who see your project, the more people who'll pledge to support it. So it's in your project's best interest for as many people as possible to know about it. This means starting your promotion before your project goes live and continuing it while the campaign is running.

I'm using the word "promote" to mean all of the efforts to increase awareness for your project, both online and offline in the real world.

In both online and offline venues, promotion works best if you already have some kind of connection to the people you're trying to engage—often called your "target audience" in business and marketing-speak.

Family and friends are the first people who usually get promoted to because you know them personally. It's comfortable and easy to tell them about what you're doing.

After that, think of other people you have a relationship with at your school, work, church, gym, club—wherever you meet people because of a shared interest. They may not be close friends, but you have more of a connection to them than a random person off the street.

Promoting to strangers is more difficult, but it can be done. This is when those other success factors I mentioned come into play: what your project is and how you set it up. Once a stranger sees your project, they'll decide based on the information on the project Home page and their own feelings whether or not to pledge. You have complete control over the former and no control whatsoever over the latter.

An important thing to remember is that once someone has pledged, they're no longer a stranger. As your campaign runs, ask your backers to help spread the word. You can also stress the fact Kickstarter is an all-or-nothing model—if the funding goal isn't met, no money is taken and no rewards are sent. Therefore, it benefits existing backers if they promote your project as every new backer increases the chance of having a successful project so everyone will receive their rewards.

Online Promotion

For online promotion, you can use Facebook, Twitter, Google+, blogs (yours and others), podcasts (yours and others), and websites (yours and others).

On social networks, mention your project and the link at different times of day, every few days. Whenever you do a Kickstarter update, post a link to that update. Ideally you already have a presence on the social network you're posting to, for example Facebook, so while you are promoting your project a lot, you're also posting other things and engaging with people in a way that has nothing to do with your project.

If you have a blog, great! Write a few posts talking about different aspects of your project and post them every few days during your campaign—with "every few days" defined as whenever you want, with my recommendation being at least once a week.

If you don't have a blog, that's okay. Do you know anyone who does? If so, and you can make some kind of connection with the blog's audience (which is more likely to get you a guest blog post), contact the blog owner. The information you send them should include a short overview of your project, the link to the project Home page (if your project has already launched), and why you think their audience would be interested in or benefit from hearing about your project, or a topic that ties into your project. If you can provide value independent of promoting your project, the person you're contacting has more reason to say "yes" to your request.

Same advice as above for podcasts and websites. If you own it, promote away. If you're asking for a spot in someone else's playground, try and bring some value or information other than "please pledge to my project." As noted above, make sure you can explain the connection between your project and their audience.

There's also the option to buy online ads, although unless they're specifically targeted to an audience you know is interested in your project, I wouldn't recommend that as a way to spend your time or money.

Offline Promotion

For offline promotion, ask around if you can leave a flier that gives a quick overview of your project and the link to the project Home page. If you go to a meeting/event/group activity where you think the people involved would be interested in hearing about your project, talk about it and hand out those fliers.

Basically, when you have a chance to tell people about your project, do.

Promotion On Kickstarter

In addition to showing up in the category you chose, your project will also show up on three other webpages on the Kickstarter website, and has the potential to show up on a few other pages as well. Each of these pages is a chance for someone who has no connection to you to find your project.

After your project launches, it'll show up on the Recently Launched page and the city search results page for the project location. Near the end of your campaign, your project will be listed on the Ending Soon page.

Recently Launched

People can get to the Recently Launched page from the list of links on the Discover page, which is a link in the Kickstarter header.

For those who like to browse Kickstarter, the Recently Launched page lets them know about new projects. Since projects go live throughout the day, every day, your project may not spend a lot of time near the top of this page.

City Search Results

Someone can search the Kickstarter website for all projects from a specific city. Your project will display in the results of the city you specified as the project location when you created your project Home page. Your project can get some exposure on a city search results page to people who like to shop local.

Ending Soon

The Ending Soon page displays projects whose campaigns are nearing the end—from hours to minutes to seconds left.

As your project gets closer to the end of your campaign, it'll show up on the Ending Soon page and may be found by someone looking to make a last minute pledge.

Other pages your project can show up on the Kickstarter website are as follows:

- Popular
- Staff Picks
- Most Funded
- Curated Pages
- Advanced search results pages

Popular

The "Popular" link on the Discover page lists projects across all categories. Using the advanced search parameters, someone can also see a list of projects ranked by popularity within a category or sub-category. Which projects are considered popular are based on Kickstarter algorithms which you have no control over, so don't worry about it.

Staff Picks

Staff Picks projects are chosen by people who work at Kickstarter. The Kickstarter Home page also displays the Staff Picks projects for each category. The way to be a Staff Pick is to create the best project you can because that's the only thing completely in your control.

Most Funded

The Most Funded page lists projects which brought in the most money during their campaigns. Your project will need to bring in a few million dollars to appear on this page.

Curated Pages

The ability to create a Curated Page is by invitation only from Kickstarter and is extended to "cultural organizations and institutions in creative fields: museums, film societies, record labels, publishers, creative trade organizations, educational institutions, and more." That organization can then feature a Kickstarter project that aligns with its mission, are created by alumni, etc. If you find an organization that has a Curated Page that fits with your project, it'd be worth your time to contact them to see if they would add your project.

Advanced Search Results Pages

When someone is on a category page, they're really on a search results page. Under the Kickstarter header are drop-down lists that change which projects show on the page. When the button that looks like a plus sign in a circle is clicked, the advanced search options display on an overlay. These options let people narrow the search results by how much has been pledged, what the funding goals is, and what percentage of the funding goal has been raised.

Using the advanced search options is a way for someone to narrow the kind of projects they want to see on the Kickstarter website. Your project may or may not fall into the parameters they're using.

Before You Start

Once you've decided to create a Kickstarter project, you have to do one thing, and I recommend you do a few other things right away as well.

You have to sign up for a Kickstarter account.

I recommend you back at least one project, check out projects similar to yours, check out totally different projects, and think about how to get the word out about your campaign.

Sign Up For A Kickstarter Account

The registration process for Kickstarter is simple.

1. Go to the Kickstarter website (http://www.kickstarter.com).

2. Click on the "Sign up" link in the top-right corner of the page.

3. On the Sign up page, fill out the form.

   A. Enter your full name. It's best for this to be your real name, the name you want to be known by to complete strangers not just your family and friends. Once you launch a project, you can't change this.

   B. Enter your email address. You'll receive project notifications such as updates and backer surveys, as well as copies of messages at this email address. You can change this later in your Account Settings which is accessed by clicking on your profile picture in the top-right corner.

C. Enter a password. This can also be changed later in your Account Settings.

D. Decide if you want to get Kickstarter's weekly email newsletter. If so, select the checkbox to opt-in. If not, make sure the checkbox isn't selected before you click the "Sign me up!" button. You can change your subscription preference later on the Notifications tab of your Account Settings.

A NOTE ABOUT SIGNING IN WITH FACEBOOK: You can sign up for a Kickstarter account using your Facebook account. This means you can use your Facebook credentials (your username and password) to log into Kickstarter. If you're already logged into Facebook, you can access some things in your Kickstarter account, but for other things you'll want to do, you'll still have to log in with your Kickstarter credentials.

I tried linking my FB account to my Kickstarter account and found it to be more annoying than useful. The tasks I often wanted to do required me to still log in with my Kickstarter credentials so already being logged into my Facebook account didn't save me any time or effort when working on my project. Try it out for yourself for a few days and then decide if you want to keep it that way.

If having your FB account linked to your Kickstarter account doesn't work for you, you can disconnect the accounts in your Account Settings.

Back A Project

Now that you have a Kickstarter account, I highly recommend you back at least one project. Backing a project isn't a requirement since you can put up a project even if you haven't supported any projects.

When you back a project, you gain valuable experience from the backer's perspective—from deciding which project to support, picking a specific pledge level, getting updates via email, filling out the backer survey, and receiving your rewards. You'll see how the creator runs their project and get a feel for how you, as a backer, want to be treated and kept informed. This insight will serve you well when you run your own project.

Most people become backers because they feel an emotional connection to some aspect of the project. That's why complete strangers give other complete strangers money via the Kickstarter website—it's about the rewards, but it's also about helping people accomplish something that's important to them.

On your project Home page, under your profile picture in the right column, Kickstarter will display how many projects you've created and how many you've backed.

I've backed projects in which the creator has supported many projects and some where the creator has backed zero projects. I've no evidence that pledging on other people's projects is of benefit to the success of your own Kickstarter campaign.

Personally, I like to see that a creator has backed at least one project. It makes me think they have a better understanding of what they're doing since they've been on the backer side of the process at least once.

Study Other Projects

Projects stay on the Kickstarter website forever or until there isn't a Kickstarter website any more.

You can find projects that met or exceeded their funding goals by the end of their campaign on this page on the Kickstarter website (http://www.kickstarter.com/discover/successful).

Once you've found a project that interests you, study it.

- What does the project Home page look like?
- How are the pledge levels structured?
- What information is in the updates?
- How frequently were updates posted?
- What kind of comments did backers leave?
- How did the creator respond to backers' comments?
- What were the reactions to the creator's comments?

- What updates were posted since the project ended?
- How often are updates viewable by everyone or only backers?
- Are the comments from backers after the estimated delivery date of the rewards positive or negative?

To see the history of the funding during a project's campaign, you can look the project up on Kicktraq or Kickspy.

Kicktraq

Kicktraq (http://www.kicktraq.com) has some great charts which let you see what was going on with a project's funding as it happened.

Enter the project name or the project URL on the Kicktraq website to see the details for that project, such as "1000 Origami Wish Cranes" or "http://www.kickstarter.com/projects/heidi2524/1000-origami-wish-cranes".

You'll see a graph of how much money came in over the duration of the campaign (Funding Progress). You can also look at Daily Data to see which days of the week brought in the most or least amount of money. At the bottom of the page are all of the updates posted before the last day of the campaign.

Looking at the graphs and charts for various projects, you can see whether their funding was a steady rise or had a sudden sweep up at the end. It's also interesting to look at the projected funding progress compared to what actually happened.

You could also correlate if anything noticeable happened with the funding related to the updates that were posted. If funding increased before an update posted, did the update mention favorable third-party promotional efforts or link to articles that mention the project? If the funding increased after an update posted, did the update announce new add-ons or stretch goals?

Kickspy

An interesting data set that Kickspy (http://www.kickspy.com) provides that Kicktraq doesn't is the "Also Backed" information—the projects backers have supported in addition to the one you're looking at. Reviewing this kind of information is another way to find successful projects to study (EX: http://www.kickspy.com/projects/heidi2524/1000-origami-wish-cranes/also-backed).

As on the Kicktraq website, you can browse or search for a project. If you do a search, be sure to review the checkboxes on the right side of the page and select the ones you want, otherwise you'll only see projects that are currently live. By selecting the "All" checkbox, your search will also include completed, canceled, and suspended projects.

Look at Similar Projects

Every Kickstarter project is associated with a category and, optionally, a sub-category. Once you know which category and sub-category is best for your project, I recommend you review other projects in that same category and sub-category.

See what their pledge levels are, how they use images, what kind of information they put in their project description and what their videos are like. One of the great things about Kickstarter is there are hundreds of examples of how to create a project live on the website all the time.

You'll have family and friends pledge to your Kickstarter because they want to support you—and your project.

Complete strangers will pledge because they want to support the project—and you. Because those people don't know you personally, however, they may be comparing your project to other projects in the same category and sub-category when deciding where to pledge their money.

Compared to other projects, is your funding reason clear? Will someone looking at your project Home page understand what they'll receive as a reward at each pledge level? Are there images in the main description to break up the text?

You don't have to create your project to look exactly like the other projects, but you should have some idea what information similar projects are presenting to their backers so you can consider addressing those areas as well.

Look At Totally Different Projects

In addition to looking at projects in your project's category and sub-category, I highly recommend looking at projects in completely different categories and sub-categories.

The purpose of reviewing totally different types of projects is that they may be doing something you've never considered or seen in projects similar to yours.

How do they use headlines in their project description? What do they cover in the "Risks and challenges" section? How many updates do they send?

Each project is unique to the creator, and there are some very creative projects on Kickstarter. Take a look at how a bunch of different projects are presented, and you may find an example of something great to do for yours.

Think About Promotion

Having the best project Home page in the world won't guarantee the project will fund.

Making sure you get the word out about your project won't guarantee your project will fund either, but you've got a much better chance if you do some promotion. The "Factors Of A Successful Project" section has some specific suggestions and you can always search online for articles about how other projects handled that aspect of their campaign. I mention it here because you really do need to think about how to get the word out before you start working on your project Home page and definitely before your project goes live.

Do you have a blog, website, podcast, YouTube channel, email list? Do you have a presence on one or more of the social media sites (Facebook, Twitter, Google+, etc.)? Are you going to any real world events where the audience would be interested in your project and you could put out fliers/bookmarks/postcards/stickers? Do your friends or family have a venue they'd let you use such as a physical store or weekly get-together where you could be a guest speaker? Where can you talk about your project to those who would be interested in hearing about it?

It's also a good idea to actually do a little promoting before your project launches. A Facebook post or tweet about how you just finished your video or a hint of the cool rewards you're working on are examples of the kind of things you could do even when you don't have a live project available.

If you have a website, you can put up a page about your project. Put an email sign-up form on it and use that URL in your promotions. Then, when your project is live, update that webpage with the link to your project Home page.

If you have a physical location that will let you promote your project, you can give out fliers with the name of your project so people can search for it once it's up on the Kickstarter website.

Those are a few suggestions of things you can do online and offline to increase awareness and raise interest in your project before it starts. Depending on your project and your personal connections, you likely have other promotional options, all of which can help you have a great start to your campaign.

Anatomy Of A Kickstarter Project

Once live on the Kickstarter website, your project is actually a mini-website of four pages: the project Home page, the Updates page, the Backers page, and the Comments page. I want to review these first so you'll know what information shows up where, what you can control, and what you can't.

You'll use the Project Tabs to put in the content for your project Home page, however I think it's important to look at that webpage from a potential backer's perspective first. Thinking of the project Home page as a whole, compared to the small segments of information you put into the Kickstarter website, is a good exercise to help you craft a comprehensive and unified presentation. The better your project Home page, the more likely someone will pledge.

You can also start to create your project Home page's content now, as there are some tasks on the Kickstarter website that can take a few days to a week to finish, such as connecting to the payment processor which is an external company from Kickstarter.

I'll also include specifications about each piece of content on the project Home page so you'll know what's needed and what's optional, as well as notes or recommendations.

As an example, I'll use my "1000 Origami Wish Cranes" project (http://www.kickstarter.com/projects/heidi2524/1000-origami-wish-cranes).

Common Elements

To start off, I'll go over the common elements that display on all of your project's pages, in addition to the standard Kickstarter header and footer:

- Project title
- Creator
- Navigation
- Project location
- Category

Project Title

Your project title displays in large centered text under the Kickstarter header. My project title was "1000 Origami Wish Cranes."

You have a maximum of 60 characters, including spaces, to title your project. Your project title should give a potential backer a general idea of what your project is about.

Try and include a basic noun such as film, book, comic, etc. in your project title. This will help people who see your project outside of its category, such as on the Discover page (http://www.kickstarter.com/discover), easily identify what you're doing so they can decide if they want to view your campaign.

Creator

The creator's name (that's you) displays under the project title. This is the name you typed in when you created your Kickstarter account. You can change this as many times as you want until you launch a project; after that it's fixed for that account.

Be sure the name you use when you launch your project is how you want to be known to family, friends, and strangers.

Navigation

There are four links in a horizontal line under your project title and creator byline. These links let people access the webpages that comprise your Kickstarter project. You don't have any control over how these display or their labels.

The four links are:

- Home
- Updates
- Backers
- Comments

Project Location

To the right of the navigation links is the project location, which is a city and state if you're in the U.S., and a city and country if you're outside the United States. The project location is a link that, when clicked, displays all of the projects on the Kickstarter website that are also identified as having that location.

You set the project location when you first create your project. It can be different than the location set in your Profile.

You can associate your project with a larger, more well-known city if your Profile location is a smaller town in that area. This way, people who browse major cities have a chance of seeing your project. Understand that your project will be one of many, many projects on those kinds of location pages, such as "Chicago, IL" which has over 3,000 projects (http://www.kickstarter.com/discover/places/chicago-il?ref=city).

If your town has several projects associated with it so that together they represent a decent sized audience who might shop local, that location page may be a better choice since your project won't have as much competition as on a major city location page. For example, "Evanston, IL" has almost 100 projects (http://www.kickstarter.com/discover/places/evanston-il?ref=city).

Category

The category or sub-category displays to the right of the project location. You define the category or sub-category when you create your project. When clicked, projects related to that category or sub-category display.

For example, a project in the Music category will display a link of "Music." A project in the sub-category of Painting, in the category of Art, will display the link "Painting."

Project Home Page

Your project Home page is the home page of the mini-website that is your project. I'm going to walk through each piece of content the backer sees on that page. Some of this content you'll provide when you create your project Home page. Some of this content Kickstarter will automatically generate and maintain for you during your campaign.

I'll also define and give specifications and notes on each of the following parts of a project Home page:

- Project image
- Project video (optional)
- Funding information

- Your profile
- Short blurb
- Project description
- Risks and challenges
- FAQ (optional, added after project is live)
- Report this project
- Pledge levels
- Funding period

Project Image

Under the project title is the project image. This is the first visual a backer sees for your project, so make it a good one.

The image must be at least 640 x 480 pixels, and can be larger if it fits a 4:3 aspect ratio which is the proportional relationship between the width and height of the image. This means a landscape image, where the width is greater than the height. Other image sizes that fit the 4:3 ratio are 800x600 and 1024x768.

The image must be saved as a JPEG (.jpg), PNG (.png), BMP (.bmp) or a GIF (.gif).

The file size of the image can't be larger than 50 MB.

The image can be changed during your campaign, so if you want, create some countdown images to put up as you near the last day (one week, 5 days, last day, etc.). This can emphasize to people coming to your project Home page that they don't have a lot of time left to pledge.

If you've uploaded a video, the backer will see a black "PLAY" button on top of your project image which, when clicked, will start the video. If you don't upload a video, the "PLAY" button won't display.

For my project image, I showed some of the origami cranes I'd folded along with the text of my project title. Because I was keeping one of the paper cranes for myself, I crossed out the "1000" and added "999." I also added the words "need a home" to show the purpose of the project and to add a story element—this wasn't just about buying a paper crane, a backer could give a Wish Crane a home.

A NOTE ABOUT THE PROJECT THUMBNAIL: You'll upload your project image on the Basics Project Tab, which I cover in the next section. Once your image is uploaded, the preview that displays to the right or at the bottom of the Basics Project Tab (depending on which browser you use) will show your project thumbnail. This is what people see on various Kickstarter pages that display many projects, such as the Popular page (http://www.kickstarter.com/discover/popular). The project image will be shrunk down to 180x135 pixels in the project thumbnail.

It's in your best interest (and your project's) for your project image to look good both on your project Home page and in your project thumbnail. Try to make the image as clear as possible so potential backers can understand what your project is about. If you have text on your project image, try to make it readable when it shows up in the project thumbnail.

Project Video

You don't need a video in order to launch your project. It is a good way to tell your story, whether you film yourself or put up a series of images to music, as I did for my Wish Cranes project.

If you decide to make a video for your project, the file size needs to be 5 GB or less.

The file format needs to be MOV, (.mov), MPEG (.mpg or .mpeg), AVI (.avi), MP4 (.mp4), 3GP (.3gp), WMV (.wmv), or FLV (.flv).

As mentioned earlier, your video footage and audio/music has to be of your own creation or licensed from someone who owns the rights. Do an online search for "royalty free music" and be sure to read the terms of use so you understand exactly what you're buying.

Some people will watch your video as soon as they hit your project Home page, so it's important to use your video to show what your project is quickly and clearly.

Your video could also be played somewhere outside of the context of your project Home page as on Facebook, YouTube, and other websites. Therefore it's important to treat your video as a mini-commercial for your project instead of something additional to the text and images in the project description. You'll want to cover who you are, why you're raising money, and what backers get as rewards.

I recommend keeping your video no longer than around five minutes, ideally two or three minutes if you can.

Once your project is live, your Dashboard will show you how many views your video gets and what percentage of those views finish watching the entire video. Be prepared that not everyone will watch your video through to the end. Around 74% percent of the people who viewed my Wish Cranes project video finished watching, which means about a quarter of the people who started the video didn't finish watching—and it was only 48 seconds long.

If you have no idea what you want to do for your video, check out other projects, from any category. See what you like, what you don't like, and what you might want to do for your own video.

Funding Information

To the right of the project image is information regarding your project's funding. You don't directly control this, however, it is the stuff you're going to obsess over during your campaign, so here's the breakdown:

- Number of backers
- Amount pledged
- Funding goal
- Countdown
- Pledge button
- Last day details

Number Of Backers

This is the total number of people who have pledged money to your project.

While watching this number go up is fun, don't spend too much energy on it. If a backer cancels their pledge, this number goes down. After your campaign ends, Kickstarter will process the pledge payments. If a payment doesn't go through and the backer doesn't fix whatever is wrong so that the payment does go through, you'll end up having fewer paid backers than the number of backers indicated.

For my Wish Cranes project, I had 271 backers pledge, then eight backers dropped because their payments didn't go through, so my total number of paid backers ended up being 263, even though 271 still displays on my project's Home page.

Amount Pledged

This is the number that's going to occupy all your attention because it shows how much money has been pledged to your project. It'll display in the currency of your country, so $ for the U.S., £ for the UK, etc.

Most of the time your Amount Pledged goes up, however it may go down if a backer cancels or reduces the amount of their pledge.

Remember, the Amount Pledged is just that, the amount of money people said they'd send you. After your campaign ends and the payments have been processed, you may not get all of that money, depending how many backers paid what they pledged. This means it's possible for you to reach your funding goal and not receive the amount of money you set out to get. If your project successfully funds, however, no matter how much money actually ends up in your bank account, you are obligated to fulfill the rewards of your project.

Funding Goal

This is how much money you need to get for your project to be considered a "success" and for you to receive the money from your backers. Pledges are processed for payment automatically by Kickstarter at the end of your campaign.

If you miss matching your funding goal by even one dollar, you won't receive any money.

Countdown

Below the funding goal, a numerical countdown displays with text below it that defines the unit of time for the number shown (days, hours, etc.). The countdown shows how much time is left before the end of your campaign.

Once you launch your project, the countdown will display in days. As you near the end of your campaign, the text under the number will switch to hours. Then minutes. Then seconds—seriously, you'll see it display how many seconds are left for your project to meet (or continue to exceed) its funding goal. And I know you'll be watching those seconds tick down.

I sure did.

Pledge Button

This is a nice big button that encourages the person looking at your project Home page to pledge.

When someone clicks on the pledge button, they're taken to a page where they can enter their pledge amount and pick a pledge level. If the person has already supported your project, clicking the pledge button will let them change the amount of money and which pledge level they want associated with their pledge, if any.

Last Day Details

This is a helpful little sentence that displays under the pledge button to note the last day of your campaign. The wording is slightly different if you haven't achieved your funding goal yet: "This project will only be funded if at least $10,000 is pledged by Tue, Apr 22, 2014 12:08 PM CST." Once you've reached your funding goal, the text will change to reflect that: "This project will be funded on Tue, Apr 22 2014 12:08 PM CST."

Once your campaign is over, that sentence no longer displays. Instead, a thin banner will show above your project image and the funding information. Within that banner is text saying whether or not your project successfully funded, did not fund, or was canceled.

Your Profile

Under the Funding Information is a block of content about you and a few links:

- Profile picture
- Your name
- Your location
- "Contact me" link
- Projects created
- Projects backed
- Facebook
- Website
- "See full bio" link

Profile Picture

Your profile picture shows up under the funding information and displays as a 100x100 pixel image. After you create your Kickstarter account, you can upload a profile picture by editing your Profile settings. Since your profile picture is used in a few places, be sure it looks good at least at a 220x220 pixel resolution. If someone clicks on your profile picture, your Profile overlay will show.

NOTE ABOUT THE PROFILE OVERLAY: Your Profile overlay shows a snapshot of the information you provided to the Kickstarter website and how many projects you've created and backed, including the following:

- Profile picture (220x220 pixels, links to your Profile page)
- Name (links to your Profile page)
- Location (links to search results that shows projects from that location)
- Date you last logged into Kickstarter (EX: "Jan 2 2014")
- Link to your full profile/bio
- Profile description
- Website links
- "Contact me" link
- Facebook link (if connected)
- Number of projects backed (when clicked, changes the Profile overlay to display large thumbnail listings of all of the

projects you've backed with links to the related projects)

- Thumbnail images and links to created projects

Your Name

The name you used when you registered for your Kickstarter account displays here. When someone clicks on your name, they'll see your Profile overlay as described above.

Some people use a nickname, and you can change your name as much as you want—until you launch a project. Once you have a live project, you can't change your name so be sure whatever is in that text field in your Profile is how you want to be known to potential backers of your current and future projects.

Your Location

Your location will display under your name.

This is your personal location, which can be different from your project's location. The information is displayed in the same format as mentioned earlier: city and state if you live in the U.S. and city and country for outside the United States.

Clicking on your location displays a search results page that shows all the projects from that location, such as Seattle, WA (http://www.kickstarter.com/discover/places/seattle-wa).

You set your location on the Profile tab of the Edit settings page. As you type in a city, Kickstarter will try and guess which one you mean and show you a list of options. You have to choose one of those real locations. This means you can't type in a made up town like "Hogsmeade," no matter how popular it is.

"Contact me" Link

Under your location is a "Contact me" link people can use to send you a message via the Kickstarter website.

When someone clicks on that link, they're asked to log into their Kickstarter account or connect via Facebook. Then they can type in their message and send it to you. You'll get an email with the contents of the message. You can also read messages related to your project on the Kickstarter website via one of the Creator Tools, which I'll talk about in the "Part 3: Run Your Campaign" section.

Projects Created

Under your profile image, Kickstarter will show how many projects you've created. If someone clicks on this number, an overlay showing large thumbnail listings of each of those projects will display and can be clicked on to go to the related project Home page—even if the campaign is over. All projects, whether or not they successfully funded, will have a listing and a link to their project Home page.

Projects Backed

Right after the Projects Created number is the number of projects you've backed. Clicking on that number will display an overlay of large thumbnail listings of all of the projects you pledged to, whether or not they funded. Each project will have a link to the related project Home page.

Facebook

If you've connected your Facebook account to your Kickstarter account, the name you use on Facebook will display as a link to your Facebook page, and the number of Friends you have will also show. If you haven't connected your Facebook account, the message "Has not connected Facebook" will display. You can connect or disconnect your FB account by going to the Edit settings page and choosing the Account tab.

Website

Under the Facebook information, one website will display (EX: heidi2524.com).

You can have more than one website link display on your Profile page, over ten links if you really want, although I wouldn't recommend it. These website links can be added, edited, and deleted on the Profile tab of the Edit settings page. Whatever website is listed first, that's the one that will display on your project Home page.

"See Full Bio" Link

Clicking on the "See full bio" link shows your Profile overlay.

Short Blurb

The short blurb displays under the project image on the project Home page as well as on the project thumbnail that displays in search results.

You have a maximum of 135 characters, including spaces, to describe your project.

Spend some time crafting your short blurb. Along with the project title and project image, the short blurb is the only piece of information potential backers see about your project when it's listed on a category page or a search results page beside a lot of other projects. Consider the short blurb the invitation to a potential backer to click through to your project Home page.

A NOTE ABOUT THE SHORT BLURB: As you fill in content on the Basics Project Tab, pay attention to how your project thumbnail looks in the preview that displays to the right or at the bottom, depending which browser you use.

Because the short blurb doesn't display in a mono-spaced font where every character has the same width, the number of characters displayed depends on the specific letters and numbers used. Depending on the words you choose, not all of your short blurb may show in your project thumbnail, even if you're using less than 135 characters.

You can see that's what happened on my Wish Cranes project if you search for "wish cranes" on the Kickstarter website. My short blurb took up 131 characters, but the last five don't show up on the project thumbnail which displays in the search results.

If not all of your short blurb displays, try different words until the project thumbnail shows all of the text you want people to see.

Project Description

The project description displays under the short blurb and to the left of the pledge levels column. The project description can contain as much text, images, videos, and audio as you want. The purpose of everything you put in the project description is to convince a potential backer to pledge their money to your creation.

The project description is the place to tell everyone who you are and what you're doing. Because some people (like me), don't watch the video until after they've read the project description, be sure to cover all of the information you mentioned in the video.

If you have rewards that are going to ship in separate packaging, like a book in a box and a poster in a tube, say so in your project description. It helps reassure backers that their rewards will arrive safely—and in the case of the poster, won't be folded to fit into a box. And be prepared to say rewards will arrive in multiple packages again in an update when you get around to shipping to try and limit the messages you get from backers about what happened to the rest of their rewards when they only receive part of what they pledged for.

The project description is also the place to reiterate your pledge levels in a visual way. The pledge levels in the right column are only text, no images can show up over there. Since you can, and often should, have images in your project description, you can create pledge graphics.

A pledge graphic is an image that shows the pledge amount and rewards in a visual way and displays in your project description.

If your project produces a book, show the cover, even if it's just a mock up—although be sure to say if any graphic you show for a reward isn't exactly what the backer will receive. For digital rewards, you can use text or an icon if appropriate. Using images, even placeholders, can often explain clearly and quickly what your rewards are and help a potential backer decide at what pledge level to support.

Pledge graphics are completely optional (I didn't have any on my Wish Cranes project) and can be as elaborate or simple as you want. Since you can change your project description during your campaign, you can update your pledge graphics as certain milestones are reached. For example, if you have pledge levels with limited quantities of rewards, you can swap out the related pledge graphic with a "Sold Out" version when those rewards are no longer available.

Pledge graphics can also be created for stretch goals. A stretch goal is a monetary amount above your project's funding goal that has a reward tied to achieving it. You can show images of the rewards for a stretch goal as a pledge graphic, or you can only show the monetary amount, then "unlock" and reveal what the rewards are by changing out the stretch goal pledge graphic with an image and description of the rewards when the stretch goal amount has been reached.

Stretch goals are optional and aren't part of the Kickstarter structure, so they don't show up in the pledge levels on the right side of the project Home page. Therefore using graphics in the main description is a good way to emphasize your stretch goals to get current and potential backers excited about reaching them.

Here are five examples of projects that used pledge graphics and stretch goal graphics to visually explain their rewards:

- Adventures for a Lazy Afternoon by Travis Hanson: http://www.kickstarter.com/projects/488571414/adventures-for-a-lazy-afternoon
- Get a custom hat, save a New York City factory: http://www.kickstarter.com/projects/satyatwena/get-a-custom-hat-save-a-new-york-city-factory
- Seven Seas Playing Cards: http://www.kickstarter.com/projects/glummies/seven-seas-playing-cards
- Torch Paddles by Creighton Baird: http://www.kickstarter.com/projects/1290122574/torch-paddles
- The 20th Anniversary Nearly Complete Essential StarChild: http://www.kickstarter.com/projects/1401678214/the-20th-anniversary-nearly-complete-essential-sta (Full disclosure: I made these pledge graphics)

A NOTE ABOUT LANGUAGE: If you know a significant part of your audience wants to read about your project in a language other than English, you can put a translated version in your project description. The "Clear And Present Thinking: A Free College-level Logic Text" project has an English and French version of their text (http://www.kickstarter.com/projects/1547922245/clear-and-present-thinking-a-free-college-level-lo).

If you do put up a translated version of your project description, make sure it accurately represents your project as you're responsible for the contents of your project Home page and for setting your backers' expectations of what they'll receive as rewards.

Risks And Challenges

Under your project description is required text where you describe the risks and challenges of your project.

This is where you reassure your potential backers that you know what you're doing, have thought of what might go wrong, and have a plan in place to deal with those misadventures.

If you have no idea what to write, check out other projects to see what things they addressed in this section. Some older projects may not have any information as this text was originally optional and only became required by Kickstarter in September 2012.

FAQ

The FAQ (frequently asked questions) text can't be added to your project Home page until after your project is live on the Kickstarter website.

Having a FAQ is optional.

If you do want to have a FAQ on your project Home page, you can add it, and add to it, at any time during your campaign. The FAQ will display as a series of collapsed links under your project description. When someone clicks on the question link, the answer will display under the question along with the date you added that entry (EX: "Sat, Jun 29 2013, 12:30 PM CST").

Under the last question link will be an "Ask a question" button. When clicked, a text box overlay will display where someone can type in a question which will be emailed to you. They must log in with their Kickstarter account or their Facebook credentials in order to send the message.

If you don't add any questions and answers, only the "Ask a question" button will display on your project Home page under the FAQ heading.

Since you can add to the FAQ at any time during your campaign, if you get questions about your project, you may want to post the answers as a FAQ in addition to replying to the individual who sent the question. If one person asks about something, it's likely a few more people out there are also wondering the same thing.

Report This Project

Under the FAQ is a "Report this project to Kickstarter" button that, when clicked, will send a message about your project to Kickstarter. The person reporting your project must provide details regarding why they're reporting your project and choose one of the following reasons:

- "This project creator is spamming me."
- "This is a charity project."
- "This is not a project."
- "Prohibited rewards."
- "I see abusive behavior on this project."
- "Intellectual property violation."

If Kickstarter decides your project is in violation of their rules (http://www.kickstarter.com/rules) or Terms of Use (http://www.kickstarter.com/terms-of-use), they can suspend your project. If your project is suspended, the campaign and funding stop. You and all of your backers are notified by email. Suspension of a project is final and can't be changed.

Pledge Levels

The right column of the project Home page, under your profile information, displays the pledge levels. This is where you tell backers what rewards they'll receive for each pledge amount. Pledge levels should be easy to scan so backers understand exactly what they get and understand how each pledge level is different from the others.

I covered the individual parts of a pledge level in the *Define Your Pledge Levels* chapter in the "Part 1: Define Your Project" section, so here I want to give some recommendations about how to craft those different aspects.

First, understand how narrow that right column really is.

There's an average of seven words per line. That means if your pledge level description has 36 words (which may not look like much when you type it out), that description will display as six lines of text on your project Home page. Do that for a bunch of pledge levels (the higher pledge levels will likely have far more words) and it gets overwhelming and difficult to parse out what exactly the backer will get.

Keep your pledge level description as succinct as possible and put all the other words into your project description. If your art book is 100, full-color pages on special paper, put all those words in the project description—and expand the text to say as much as you want about the details and uniqueness of the binding, paper, color printing process, etc. In your pledge level description, just say "book."

If your rewards are cumulative where the higher pledge levels include the rewards of lower pledge levels, you can say something along the lines of "includes lower pledge level rewards" instead of repeating all of the rewards in every pledge level description.

If you have a pledge level that includes one specific lower pledge level reward but not others, it can be useful to name each pledge level. That way you can say a pledge level includes the "Super Fan" pledge level as well as whatever reward is unique to the pledge level you're writing the description for, instead of having to also include the full text of the "Super Fan" pledge level.

It's important to keep your reward identifiers consistent, which means always use the same words to describe the same thing. Yes, it can feel repetitive, but it'll help eliminate confusion for your backers. If one of your rewards is a "graphic novel," don't refer to it as a "collection" somewhere else.

Be careful of generic terms such as "big," "mini," "full-sized," etc. Give specific sizes for your rewards, especially if you have rewards of different sizes. For example, say "mini-print (5" x 7")" not just "mini-print."

Earlier I mentioned using just the word "book" in a pledge level description. That works if you only have one version of the book. If you have more than one version, "book" becomes the generic word you want to avoid—instead use specific terms that apply to the rewards such as "hardcover" and "softcover."

If your pledge level has a criteria that must be met in order to receive the reward (EX: be a certified bookseller/retailer), put that information first in your pledge level description, whether it's as a pledge level name or just text. If the backer is seeing a truncated version of your pledge level descriptions, which is possible on a mobile device, they may or may not read the full description before pledging. Being up front about a special backer criteria that must be met in order to receive a reward can help avoid issues later in fulfillment.

Sometimes rewards are autographed and if yours fall into that category, say so in your pledge level description. Also mention if you're doing any personalization as in "To [name]." This is important for the backers to know, and for you to keep in mind because you should ask what name the reward should be personalized to when you send out the backer surveys to collect shipping and other information after your campaign is over.

For some art-related projects, a creator may offer commissioned work. If that's you, note any restrictions; for example, up to two characters, group shots of no more than four characters, no background, etc. Also note any type of content you won't do, such as characters under someone else's copyright, violent content, etc. This kind of information can be in your project description, with a text in the commissioned work pledge level description along the lines of "see project description for more details."

Give yourself some extra time when you set the estimated delivery date for commissions. You have to account for fulfilling all of the Kickstarter rewards for all of the backers, plus your regular life and your regular work load. It's okay to tell people they won't get their commission for up to a year after your campaign ends—just be sure you meet that deadline when it comes around.

Higher pledge level rewards can involve a personal touch that's more than an autograph or personalization such as a sketch, a note, a small hand-made item, etc. Ideally you set a quantity limit on this kind of reward. Limited quantities make a reward special and you'll know exactly how long it'll take you to fulfill the rewards.

Kickstarter will display your pledge levels from the smallest amount at the top of the right column down to the largest at the bottom. You can have more than one pledge level with the same pledge amount, just be sure to offer different rewards.

However you set up your pledge levels, understand this information is what most backers are primarily interested in. Help them decide which level to pledge at by being as clear and succinct as you can about what rewards they'll receive.

Funding Period

Kickstarter displays the dates of the funding period for your project under your last pledge level with the duration of the campaign listed in parentheses. For example: "Jun 14 2013 - Jul 24 2013 (31 days)."

This is a handy way to quickly see how long a campaign a project had. Since a campaign can run between 1-60 days, check out similar projects to see how long they lasted, how much money they raised in that amount of time, and whether or not they met their funding goals.

Updates Page

In addition to your project Home page, you also have a dedicated Updates page (EX: http://www.kickstarter.com/projects/heidi2524/1000-origami-wish-cranes/posts).

All updates you post about your project will show up on this page as well as get emailed to the designated backers.

The number beside the "Updates" link is how many updates you've posted. Each update is numbered, has a title, and then the message that can contain text, images, videos, and audio files.

If you post an update with the setting "Anyone," then everyone who goes to your Updates page can see the entire update.

If your update is set for only backers, just the number of the update and the title will display on the Updates page. If a backer has logged into their Kickstarter account, they'll be able to see the entire update.

Backers Page

The Backers page lists the people who have pledged to your project. The number beside the "Backers" link is your total number of backers.

Since this page only updates every time an additional ten people have pledged, the number of names displayed will be out of sync with the number shown. When you first launch your project, the Backers page will be blank until ten people have pledged.

The person's name and how many projects they've backed display in rows on the page. If the person has set a location for their profile, the city and state or city and country will also show. The backer's name is a link to their Profile page.

Comments Page

The Comments page displays comments left by your backers. Anyone can see all of the comments on this page, but only backers and you can leave comments.

During your campaign, it's a good idea to keep an eye on this page and address any issues or questions that come up. Even if you follow up via a Kickstarter message, or add a FAQ entry to your project Home page, remember to also leave a comment otherwise people who review this page won't know that the issue was addressed. Commenting yourself on this page, even just to thank people for taking the time to leave comments, is a good way to directly engage with your backers.

FOUR PARTS OF A KICKSTARTER PROJECT

Creating a Kickstarter project is a huge effort and there are a lot of details to keep track of, but not all of those details are important all of the time. In order to help you prioritize, I've divided the process of doing a project into four parts:

1. **Define your project** by picking a category, determining your budget, setting up your pledge levels, thinking about your stretch goals, and developing a timeline.

2. **Create your project** using the Kickstarter website, ask for feedback on your Preview, then launch your project or ask a Kickstarter Community Manager for advice.

3. **Run your campaign** by promoting your project, maintaining your project Home page, sending updates, and communicating with your backers.

4. **Fulfill your promises** by getting rewards made, sending out the backer surveys, using your backer report spreadsheets, and shipping the rewards.

Each of these parts gets a dedicated section because there's a lot to cover.

Part 1: Define Your Project

In order to have a successful Kickstarter project, enough people need to pledge enough money to reach your funding goal. It's simple, and like most simple things, takes some carefully crafted effort to achieve.

The best way to engage people to give their money is to communicate as clearly as possible what the project is. In order to do that, you have to go through the following tasks to define your project:

- Pick your project category
- Determine your funding goal
- Define your pledge levels
- Create a timeline

I've talked a bit about each of these tasks before, and now it's time to go over the details.

Pick Your Project Category

You need to help people understand what your project is because people don't fund what they don't understand.

Kickstarter provides a list of categories to help give a big picture idea of your project. All of the categories have sub-categories to help define your project even further and get you closer to your potential backers.

You can see a list of Kickstarter's categories on their Home page (http://www.kickstarter.com) and I've listed them here, along with the related sub-categories:

- **Art** - Ceramics, Conceptual Art, Digital Art, Illustration, Installations, Mixed Media, Painting, Performance Art, Public Art, Sculpture, Textiles, Video Art
- **Comics** - Anthologies, Comic Books, Events, Graphic Novels, Webcomics
- **Crafts** - Candles, Crochet, DIY, Embroidery, Glass, Knitting, Letterpress, Pottery, Printing, Quilts, Stationery, Taxidermy, Weaving, Woodworking
- **Dance** - Performances, Residencies, Spaces, Workshops
- **Design** - Architecture, Civic Design, Graphic Design, Interactive Design, Product Design, Typography
- **Fashion** - Accessories, Apparel, Childrenswear, Couture, Footwear, Jewelry, Pet Fashion, Ready-to-wear
- **Film & Video** - Action, Animation, Comedy, Documentary, Drama, Experimental, Family, Fantasy, Festivals, Horror, Movie Theaters, Music Videos, Narrative Film, Romance, Science Fiction, Shorts, Television, Thrillers, Webseries
- **Food** - Bacon, Community Gardens, Cookbooks, Drinks, Events, Farms, Farmer's Markets, Food Trucks, Restaurants, Small Batch, Spaces, Vegan
- **Games** - Gaming Hardware, Live Games, Mobile Games, Playing Cards, Puzzles, Tabletop Games, Video Games
- **Journalism** - Audio, Photo, Print, Video, Web
- **Music** - Blues, Chiptune, Classical Music, Country & Folk, Electronic Music, Faith, Hip-Hop, Indie Rock, Jazz, Kids, Latin, Metal, Pop, Punk, R&B, Rock, World Music

- **Photography** - Animals, Fine Art, Nature, People, Photobooks, Places
- **Publishing** - Academic, Anthologies, Art Book, Calendars, Children's Book, Fiction, Literary Journals, Nonfiction, Periodical, Poetry, Radio & Podcast, Translations, Young Adult, Zines
- **Technology** - 3D Printing, Apps, Camera Equipment, DIY Electronics, Fabrication Tools, Flight, Gadgets, Hardware, Makerspaces, Robots, Software, Sound, Space Exploration, Wearables, Web
- **Theater** - Experimental, Festivals, Immersive, Musical, Plays, Spaces

Your project has to fit into one of the above. With that out of the way, your project Home page can give potential backers the details of what makes your project unique within that category.

If you think more than one category or sub-category is appropriate for your project, check out those areas on the Kickstarter website—all of the categories are listed at the bottom of every Kickstarter webpage. Once you're in a category, you can click on the category name in the search options at the top of the page to see the related sub-categories. Which category or sub-category has projects that are most like yours? Use that one.

A NOTE ABOUT TAGS: If you're on a search results page or a category page and click on the plus icon in a circle at the top of the page, you'll see an overlay with more search options, including tags.

Examples of tags are "Cats," "Open source," "Science," "Zombies," etc. Tags are independent of a category which means projects with the "#zombies" tag could be in "Art," or "Dance," or "Technology." Tags are created and applied to projects by Kickstarter staff as of the beginning of 2013.

As a creator, you don't have any control over what tag is applied to your project or if a tag is assigned at all. You can contact Kickstarter with a tag suggestion via Twitter (http://twitter.com/kickstarter). In the future, creators may be able to assign tags to their project.

Determine Your Funding Goal

One of the important aspects of a Kickstarter project that's different from some other crowdfunding websites is that money is collected from the backers only if the funding goal is reached. This means if your funding goal is $1,000 and only $999 is pledged by the end of the campaign, your project is considered unsuccessful. No money will be taken from the backers and no money will be deposited into your bank account.

If your project doesn't fund, you can create a new project that's similar and try again. I've seen this happen at least twice—once where the second project was almost exactly the same as the first, and one where the second project was only somewhat similar to the original project.

It's preferable that your first project fund, however, so it's important you spend some time figuring out your funding goal.

The funding goal is the total amount of money your project must raise and can be any amount from under $100 to millions of dollars. There are no fixed or set dollar amounts for projects because every creator's project is unique.

For example, a project for a book may have editing and cover art and printing expenses. Creating a CD might need money to pay musicians and the recording facility. A fashion project could raise money to have a limited series of prototypes created for a show. Each of those projects will have a funding goal unique to the expenses and rewards related to that project.

The funding goal should cover the following:

- Project expenses
- Reward costs
- Packaging and shipping
- Fees (Kickstarter and payment processor)
- Taxes

Project Expenses

How much money is it going to take to finish your project?

Project expenses are often independent of reward costs. For example, the project expense of paying an artist to draw a comic book doesn't cover the reward cost of printing the comic book. You may or may not decide to include licensing costs for content used to create your project Home page in your funding goal as well.

Make a list of every project expense you can think of. Each of those expenses likely has a range from a lower "this gets the job done" number to a higher "this is the dream" number. Add up the lower and higher numbers from each expense and you'll have a range of your project expenses to use in calculating your funding goal.

Reward Costs

How much money will it take to create the project's rewards?

In many cases, the reward costs depend on the quantity and quality of the reward produced. You'll have to play with the numbers to find a balance between how many rewards you need to produce, how much money it'll cost to produce them, and how much you think a backer would pay for them.

As you define your reward costs, you're also helping define your pledge levels, which determine how much money a backer will pledge in expectation of the related reward.

Reward costs are often the most difficult numbers to figure out. Again, take a look at similar projects and see if they have limits on their rewards, or if the creator shared the quantities of what they wanted to produce in their project description.

Packaging And Shipping

If you're creating physical rewards such as a book, a CD, or art prints, you have to ship them to your backers. Pay attention to this because shipping costs can eat up a lot of your funding goal if you're not careful.

Before you can ship a reward, you need to pack it in something the shipping service of your choice will accept. What size envelopes or boxes are you going to use? Are the envelopes padded? What kind of filler do you need in the boxes to make sure your rewards arrive undamaged? How much tape are you going to need to seal the boxes? Does the shipping service you plan to use provide any free packaging materials?

Once you know how you're going to package the reward, you can figure out an estimate of how much it'll cost to ship.

A NOTE ON STRETCH GOALS: Some projects have a very low entry pledge level (EX: $1), that doesn't have any physical or digital rewards since it's used as a way for a backer to show support for the project with minimal financial commitment.

If your stretch goal (a monetary goal higher than your funding goal) involves a physical reward for "all pledge levels," however, there is now a shipping cost associated with every backer at the $1 level. Depending what the stretch goal reward is, and where the backer lives, their $1 pledge may not cover the packaging and shipping cost now needed. If you have a $1 pledge level, be very careful about having a stretch goal with a physical reward that goes to "all pledge levels" as you could end up with packaging and shipping costs you didn't account for and have to pay for them out of your own pocket.

A NOTE ABOUT ADD-ONS: Depending how you structure your pledge levels, you may want to allow backers to add individual rewards to their pledges. For example, a pledge level could be a DVD, and the add-on could be a poster. Add-ons are great for your backers as they can get exactly what they want. Keep in mind that add-ons can be a headache for you as they affect the size and weight of the packages to be shipped.

If you allow add-ons, be prepared to possibly need extra packaging to accommodate them, and try to estimate what the additional shipping costs will be.

Size

The shipping size is usually defined by length, width, and height. Even an envelope can incur an extra charge if its height is above a certain thickness—this happened to me on my Wish Cranes project. Folded paper cranes, even when laid flat, are still too thick for the basic rate of First Class mail, so there was an additional 20 cent charge per envelope.

In some cases, you may end up shipping rewards of different sizes to the same backer. If the size of the individual rewards are better suited to different types of packaging, you may want to consider mailing multiple packages. You could save money using packaging specific to the shape of each reward instead of using a single package. For example, a small box for a DVD and a tube for a rolled poster, compared to a single box large enough to accommodate the poster and a lot of padding so the DVD doesn't move around and get damaged.

Weight

If you don't have an example of your reward available, use something similar to the reward you're going to ship to estimate the weight. Weight definitely plays a factor in the shipping costs. Some shipping services have ready-made packaging with an associated maximum weight, such as "4 pounds and 20 ounces" or "up to 70 lbs." Do some comparisons and see how the prices compare to using your own packaging and paying for a specific weight.

And if you're shipping paper, understand paper is heavy. That 600 page book is going to have a hefty shipping cost, especially internationally.

Distance

For each reward level, you can designate whether or not you'll only ship to backers in your country, or if you'll ship to anyone in the world. Even if a foreign destination is closer to you than a destination in your own country, some shipping services will charge extra because that package is going across a border and is therefore considered "international."

Speed

The faster you want a package to arrive, the more it will cost. Different shipping services have different costs for similar speeds, so do some research to determine the best balance between speed, cost, and meeting your backers' expectations for the delivery of their rewards. Also, if you're shipping multiple packages, it may save you some money to ship the heavier packages slower than the lighter ones.

Tracking Information

One thing to consider is whether or not you'll provide tracking information to your backers for their reward packages. Depending on which shipping service and methods you use, tracking may be part of what you're already paying for, or it may be an additional cost. The replacement cost of a reward is also a consideration—it may be worth paying to track an $800 piece of art but not a $10 CD.

Backers love tracking information because they can see their rewards en route.

Tracking information can be great for creators because it allows them to provide an accurate answer to the inevitable backer question of "Where's my reward?"

You'll have to take a look at the costs involved, both financial and emotional, and determine if it's worth having tracking information for your reward packages.

Online Shipping Calculators

Sometimes you can find the information you need online from the shipping service website, sometimes it may be worth your time to visit a shipping facility and talk to someone about what you want to do. Since most shipping calculators need a destination to give an estimate, pick some example destinations, both domestic and foreign.

Since I live in Texas, if I use a New York zip code and a California zip code as destinations in an online shipping calculator, I'll get a good idea of how much it'd cost to send a reward to either coast, and I can assume the states in between will probably cost less. Internationally, Australia is as far as something can go from me, and Germany is a good estimate for rewards going to Europe.

Kickstarter doesn't have a mechanism to add an additional shipping costs for backers in your own country, therefore the shipping costs for their rewards have to be accounted for elsewhere—either in the pledge level amount, the general funding goal, or out of your own pocket.

International Shipping Fee

For each pledge level, you have the option to select a checkbox and enter a suggested additional amount to help cover the shipping costs for backers outside your country. Kickstarter will display this amount as text under the pledge level's estimated delivery date, as in "Add $20 to ship outside the US."

This additional amount is not enforced by Kickstarter. It's up to each international backer to add that amount to their pledge. It's also a flat fee for all international backers—the Kickstarter website won't let you use that functionality to add $10 for people in one country and $30 for people in a different country.

If you want to offer different additional shipping amounts based on a backer's country, you have two options:

- Ask for different international shipping amounts
- Create country-specific pledge levels.

Ask For Different International Shipping Amounts

In this case, don't use that "additional shipping" checkbox when you create your pledge levels. Instead, add text and a map to your project description to explain the different international shipping costs. Then, in every pledge level that needs it, put text along the lines of "See main description for international shipping costs." or specifically list the different costs, as in "Please add $15 for shipping to Canada & Mexico and $20 for all other non-US countries."

Here are two examples of projects who took that approach:

- Tanner Jones and the Quest for the Monkey Stone: http://www.kickstarter.com/projects/488571414/tanner-jones-and-the-quest-for-the-monkey-stone
- Cartoonist Mike Kunkel's Squiggle Art Book!: http://www.kickstarter.com/projects/149368010/mike-kunkels-squiggle-project

Create Country-specific Pledge Levels

To do this, be sure your pledge description is very clear that only people from certain countries should back at that pledge level. You can then wrap the international shipping cost into the pledge amount and not have to worry about whether backers add the additional money on their own. The "Masters of Anatomy" project used this method for the hardcover and softcover versions of their book (http://www.kickstarter.com/projects/1302528630/masters-of-anatomy).

Online Shipping Services

Each online shipping service will have their own fee structure. Some may require you to purchase or lease a specific kind of printer and labels. Depending how many packages you have to ship, such a service may ultimately save you time and money.

For creators in the United States, the U.S. Post Office offers discounted rates for some shipping services if the postage is purchased online.

Fees

There are two kinds of fees that will be taken out of the total amount of money your project raises if it's successful: the Kickstarter fee, and the payment processor fee.

The Kickstarter fee is 5%, an easy amount to estimate. If your project doesn't meet its funding goal, you don't pay this fee. Assuming your project reaches its funding goal, you pay this fee on the final amount collected from your backers.

The payment processor fee varies by the company who collects the pledge money and that varies by the creator's country. You can look up the details for each country on the Fees page of the Kickstarter website (http://www.kickstarter.com/help/fees).

For the U.S., the payment processor fee can be 3-5%

For the clients I work with, I tell them to estimate 10% to account for the Kickstarter and payment processor fees. The estimate may end up being a bit high, but it won't be low, which is the important part.

Adding Up Your Estimates

Now that you have a pretty good idea of your project expenses, reward costs, how much money it'll cost for packaging and shipping, and fees, add up those numbers to get your funding goal.

Do you think enough people will pledge to reach that amount?

If not, are there places you can lower some of the costs? How much of your own money can you contribute? Are there people who would help you financially, independent of the Kickstarter project?

You can also look at other projects in your category to see how your funding goal compares. Your project doesn't have to have a similar funding goal as other projects, but this exercise will give you an idea of which dollar amounts tend to get funded, and which don't.

A NOTE ABOUT TAXES: According to the Kickstarter website, funds raised by a project are generally subject to taxes.

How much you'll be taxed is based on a lot of variables including your other income, where you live, how much money your project raised, and your project expenses.

Therefore, there's no information in this book related to how much tax you'll pay on the money your project raises because I have no clue.

Your best bet is to consult with your accountant, especially if your funding goal is in the thousands of dollars range, or you think you might raise that much.

Kickstarter provides a guide for your accountant that covers the basics to help them understand where the money came from (http://www.kickstarter.com/help/taxes). It's a webpage, so you may want to print it out for your accountant. There are also links to tax authority websites for a few countries in addition to the United States listed at the bottom.

A NOTE ABOUT NONPROFITS: If you are a nonprofit organization, and your project will produce something, not just raise money for your cause, you can use Kickstarter and you may be able to offer your backers tax deductions. Kickstarter has more information about this on their Creator Questions FAQ (http://www.kickstarter.com/help/faq/creator+questions#faq_41842).

Define Your Pledge Levels

Most projects have multiple pledge levels so backers have options of how much money to give in support. Lower pledge levels often have smaller/fewer/less expensive rewards than higher amount pledge levels. A backer doesn't have to pick a pledge level. They can just pledge money in support of your project and choose not to receive any rewards.

You can have one pledge level or over 20 pledge levels. Just remember you'll have to send a backer survey for each pledge level, and each pledge level will have its own backer report spreadsheet of information once the project has successfully funded. The more pledge levels you have, the more work you'll have in fulfillment.

Since you've worked through your reward costs as part of determining your funding goal, you have a good idea of what you want your rewards to be, which is important, as every pledge level has to have some kind of reward.

I'll go over the information needed to create a pledge level, then talk about stretch goals.

Pledge Level Parts

Every pledge level consists of the following information:

- Pledge amount
- Description
- Rewards
- Estimated delivery date
- Shipping details
- Limit quantity (optional)

Pledge Amount

The pledge amount is how much money you ask a backer to spend in return for the specified reward.

The pledge amount for U.S. projects has to be at least $1, can't be more than $10,000, and has to be in whole dollar amounts. Other countries may have other limits and the Kickstarter website will let you know what they are when you fill out that section of the project Home page.

As mentioned earlier, you can have the same pledge amount for different pledge levels if you wish. In that case, the rewards should be different and that difference should be clearly noted in the description.

Description

The description of the pledge level tells the backer what they'll receive in return for supporting the project at that amount. You don't have to mention the pledge amount, as Kickstarter will display that for you above the pledge description.

Some projects give each pledge level a name and list it in the description. For example, "Fan," "Biggest Fan," "Super Fan," etc. Using a name can make it easier for people to differentiate your pledge levels from each other, especially if the pledge levels have the same pledge amount. As an example, there could be $125 "Super Fan" pledge level and a $125 "Bookseller" pledge level.

You should mention if a pledge level includes the rewards from previous pledge levels either by listing those individual rewards again, or using a phrase such as "includes rewards from all lower pledge levels," or use the name of a specific pledge level as in "includes Biggest Fan rewards."

For now, think about how you want to describe your pledge levels and what images you could use to show backers what they'll get; people really like seeing images of their rewards.

Rewards

For each pledge level, you promise to give the backer a reward, which can be just about anything. Kickstarter does have a list of prohibited things that can't be rewards (http://www.kickstarter.com/rules/prohibited), so be sure to review that before you start.

Whatever your rewards, they should be related in value to the amount pledged at that level. People understand the reason for a Kickstarter project is to raise money, so a certain amount of overage is expected, however you probably aren't going to get many pledges if the amount of money asked for is significantly higher than the perceived value of the reward. For example, you'll likely get more pledges at $5 than $10 for a single MP3.

Estimated Delivery Date

The estimated delivery date is the month and year you promise the backer will have their rewards. You can set the year to the current year, or any year up to five years out. Each pledge level can have a different estimated delivery date if you want. Working out your timeline will help you establish the estimated delivery dates for your rewards.

Shipping Details

There are three ways to tell your backers how you'll ship the rewards:

- Shipping anywhere in the world

- Shipping within your country only
- No shipping involved

Shipping Anywhere In The World

This means what it says—you'll ship rewards anywhere your backers might live, whatever it may cost to do so.

If you select this option for your pledge level, you'll have the option to select a checkbox to add an additional fee for international orders. This additional international shipping fee will display under the pledge level description, but understand it's up to the backer to add that amount to their pledge. This is the extra shipping fee mentioned earlier that Kickstarter doesn't automatically add to a backer's pledge—although international backers will get a text prompt to add more money to cover shipping when they make their pledge.

Shipping Within Your Country Only

If you choose this one, you're telling your backers that you'll only ship the reward to them if they live in the same country as you do, so domestic shipping only. It's totally cool if you want to do that. International backers can still pledge to your project if they wish.

No Shipping Involved

This option should be used if you aren't going to mail a physical reward. The reward could be electronic, such as a PDF, MP3, link to a video, etc., or intangible, as in a $1 pledge of gratitude. The point is the reward doesn't require packaging and shipping, although an estimated delivery date is still required.

Limit Quantity

Any pledge level can be set to a predetermined quantity. Kickstarter will display the text "Limited ([A] left of [B])" under the pledge amount, where [A] will be the number of pledges still available out of [B], the total number set as the limited quantity, for example "(24 left of 50)."

This means there are only a certain number of rewards available for the duration of the campaign. Once that many people have pledged to that level, it'll be marked as "All gone!" and no one else will be allowed to get that reward. If a backer changes their pledge to a different level or cancels it, Kickstarter automatically removes the "All gone!" label and again displays how many pledges are available out of the total quantity.

You can increase or decrease the limited quantity, or even remove it for a pledge level during your campaign.

Not that you're likely to have a limit this high, but just so you know, as of December 2013, the maximum number you can enter for a limited quantity is 2,147,483,647.

Pledge Amounts And Rewards

While some backers pledge just to help out, most backers pledge at a certain level because they want the related reward. Your task is to balance the pledge amount with what rewards you offer to please your backers and cover your costs, including shipping.

Since the rewards are linked to what your project is about, you probably already have an idea of what you want the rewards to be such as a book, a CD, etc. Start with a single item and assign it a pledge amount. Then work through lower and higher pledge amounts until you're happy with the range of pledge levels.

For example, a CD could be $12 while a single song/MP3 could be $3 and two CDs could be $20. A printed book could be $15 while the PDF is $5 and the book and the PDF are $18.

Also think if there are ways you can provide electronic versions of your physical items—desktop wallpaper of an art print, a PDF of a CD booklet with lyrics for people who pledge for an MP3 album, etc. These electronic rewards could be part of the related pledge level or available on their own as a lower pledge level. Be creative and interesting with your rewards as this is a key way to differentiate your project.

A NOTE ABOUT THE $1 PLEDGE: For most projects, I recommend having a $1 pledge level with a reward of "gratitude." While $1 pledges may not contribute that much to your funding goal, it's a way for people to show their support and receive updates about the project since they're officially a backer. Backers at every pledge level will receive your project updates via email unless they choose to change that setting in their Kickstarter profile.

I'll also tell you that for my Wish Cranes project I didn't have a $1 pledge level because my first pledge level amount was $3 to receive one paper crane. Those two pledge amounts were close enough that I decided not to offer a $1 pledge.

As with almost everything about your project, it's up to you to decide what you want to do, including whether or not you want to offer a $1 pledge level.

Add-Ons / A La Carte Items

If you have extra items you'd like your backers to have the option to pay for, but don't want to wrap them up into a specific pledge level, you can have one or more add-on or a la carte items. A backer can choose which extra item they want by adding a specific monetary amount to their existing pledge.

You can see an example of extra items on this project: http://www.kickstarter.com/projects/149368010/mike-kunkels-squiggle-project.

Add-ons can be limited to only certain pledge levels, or you can allow any backer at any pledge level to have any add-on. It's completely up to you.

Add-ons are very convenient for your backers in that they can get exactly what they want. Add-ons can be a massive headache for you during fulfillment in that there is no record of what backer has paid for which add-on. You have to rely on your backers to tell you which add-ons they ordered via the backer survey, or message, or email, or however you collect information for fulfillment. You then have to verify that the amount of money they sent covers their pledge level as well as the cost of the add-on they said they ordered.

Stretch Goals

As mentioned earlier, a stretch goal is a monetary amount above your project's funding goal that has related rewards. If the stretch goal is reached before the end of your campaign, you'll add the related rewards to whatever rewards the backer will receive based on their pledge level.

Stretch goals evolved outside the Kickstarter process so there is no designated place to enter your stretch goals when creating your project Home page. Most creators list their stretch goals in the project description, often using pledge graphics.

Stretch Goal Amount

You can set your stretch goal amount to be whatever you want, closer or more of a stretch from your funding goal. You can have as many stretch goals as you want. Just remember, every stretch goal is an extra promise you have to fulfill.

As an example, if your funding goal is $1,000, your first stretch goal amount could be $1,500 or it could be $2,000 or $5,000. Your stretch goals could be at set intervals (EX: $1,500, $2,000, $2,500), or be completely random (EX: $11,234, $29,402, $35,000).

Personally, I find stretch goals that are relatively close to each other more fun and exciting as the possibility of reaching them is higher and therefore more interesting to potential and existing backers.

Your initial funding goal, the pledge amounts of your pledge levels, and how large of an existing audience you have are also factors to consider when planning for stretch goals.

An important part of determining your stretch goal amounts is to evaluate what the rewards will be and what pledge levels they will apply to if your project reaches those levels of over-funding.

Stretch Goal Rewards

As with the rewards for pledge levels, stretch goal rewards can be almost anything. Here are some examples of stretch goals I've seen on Kickstarter projects:

- Improve the quality of an existing reward (EX: add slipcase to a hardcover book)
- Add content to an existing reward (EX: new, never before-seen comic added to the collection)
- Increase production quantities (EX: print an extra 2,000 copies of a book)
- Add new rewards (EX: art print for pledge levels $15 and higher)
- Increase number of existing rewards (EX: get two DVDs when pledge level was originally for one)
- Make available a new add-on (EX: an extra figurine for $10)

Stretch goal rewards can go to everyone, or only selected backers by calling out specific pledge levels as in "pledge levels $15 and higher."

You can also have a stretch goal reward that goes to your backers in one format and have that same item in a different format as an add-on. For example, a stretch goal reward could be a short story that's delivered as an ebook to all backers and the printed version of that same short story could be a $5 add-on. This way you reward your backers with the free ebook for helping the project reach a stretch goal. For those who want a printed version, the cost of the production, packaging, and shipping is covered by the add-on amount.

Remember when you say a stretch goal will result in a physical reward for "all pledge levels" that it includes your $1 pledge level (if you have one), and you may incur shipping costs that weren't previously accounted for.

A NOTE ABOUT STRETCH GOALS: As a backer, I personally like to see stretch goals or at least read a mention of them as it indicates the creator has thought about what might happen if their project brings in more money than their funding goal.

I'll also tell you that for my Wish Cranes project I didn't have any stretch goals as there were only 1000 folded pieces of paper to ship out, and I didn't want to deal with creating other rewards.

So know that whether or not your project has stretch goals is entirely up to you.

Create A Timeline

One of the last things, and a significantly important thing, to help your project be a success is to figure out your timeline.

Your timeline shows what dates you expect things to get done. There's a list of ten important dates I think you should define for your project which will help you set the estimated delivery date for getting the rewards to your backers.

First, however, I want to cover the concepts of Work and Duration, and the Scotty Principle—you don't need to be a Star Trek fan for it to work for you.

Work And Duration

In order to create a timeline for your project, from adding content to your project Home page through shipping the rewards, you need to know how long it takes for things to happen. The "how long" part is actually two numbers: Work and Duration.

Work is the number of hours it takes to do the actual task.

For example, I timed myself folding an origami crane and it took about six minutes. I'd folded 400 cranes and had 600 more to go before I could ship them, so that's 3,600 minutes which is 60 hours. So the Work required was 60 hours.

Duration is how many days it will take you to do the Work.

Even if I could spend eight hours a day folding origami cranes to get the Work done in just over a week, those would be crazy days of monotonous labor that might even cause a repetitive strain injury. Not going to happen. I could, however, spend one hour an evening folding origami cranes, which means it'd take me 60 days. So my Duration could be considered 60 days for producing the rewards for my project.

But, looking at my schedule, I had family vacation and travel coming up and knew there wouldn't be any crane folding happening on those days. So instead of two months,

I set my Duration to four months.

The Work was 60 hours and the Duration was four months, which is about 2,928 hours.

Hopefully you now see why it's important to create your timeline based on Duration, not Work.

Most people are pretty good about knowing how much Work it'll take to produce what's needed for their project, since most Kickstarter projects are in some way their passion.

Guessing at the Duration while making sure you have enough time to create, order, pack, and ship all of the rewards with everything else you already have going on in your life is more of a challenge. That's why I want to mention the Scotty Principle.

The Scotty Principle

The Scotty Principle is named in honor of Montgomery "Scotty" Scott, the engineer on the original Star Trek TV Show. Scotty was considered a miracle worker because he always finished fixing the ship earlier than his estimates.

> Scotty: "I'll need four hours to get the engines back online."
>
> Captain Kirk: "You have three."
>
> [Scotty gets the engines online in two.]

In Scotty's case, his use of this principle saved the Enterprise and earned him much appreciation.

In your case, it's going to save your sanity and keep your backers happy.

This is how you apply the Scotty Principle to your project:

A. Create your time estimates

B. Add extra time for circumstances you think might delay delivery

C. Add a bit more time for potential circumstances you can't even conceive of right now

D. Use that as your estimated delivery date

E. Deliver early because some of B and/or C didn't happen

If some of B and/or C happens, you have the time to deal with it without having to tell your backers their rewards will be late.

If all of B and C and even more things happen, and you'll end up delivering late, tell your backers as soon as you know. People are a lot more willing to accept a delay if they're told it's going to happen before it happens.

Most people realize Kickstarter is not a store, that it's a venue to recruit financial supporters for creative projects. And creative projects can sometimes run screaming over their deadline with their hair on fire.

You have complete control over what information appears for each pledge level, so it's entirely up to you to manage your backers expectations by putting out an estimated delivery date you can meet. Or ideally, get ahead of, which is why employing the Scotty Principle is an important part of creating your timeline.

Ten Timeline Dates

Now that you have an understanding of Work, Duration, and the Scotty Principle, here's that list of the ten timeline dates you should account for in your project:

1. Project content and account information
2. Get feedback and prepare for launch
3. Campaign launches
4. Campaign ends
5. Money is in your back account
6. Rewards are finished
7. Send backer surveys
8. Process backer report spreadsheets
9. Start packing rewards
10. Estimated delivery date

As you read through the explanation of each timeline date, think about where those dates might fall on a calendar for your project.

Some people know the day they want their project to launch. Other creators want their rewards ready by a certain date for an event/show/concert/etc. Other people have a date to hand over files for production of the rewards.

Whatever date is significant to you, put that on a calendar and then work backward and forward to estimate the other timeline dates. The total Duration of what it takes to run a project from beginning to end may turn out to be longer than you originally thought.

Once you have that overall timeline laid out, take a good look at the days between your ten timeline dates and think about everything else you have to do that has nothing to do with your Kickstarter project. Are you traveling? Are there national holidays where you'll be spending time with friends and family? Are there international holidays which could affect the people you're working with to produce your rewards, as in Chinese New Year in February during which some businesses are closed for a week? How about your day job?

Be as realistic as you can about how much time you have available to make your project a success.

1. Project Content And Account Information

This timeline date is when you start creating your project content and filling out your account information. Both of these tasks need to be completed before your project can launch and will take some time to do. I'll go through how to accomplish them in detail in the next section, "Part 2: Create Your Project." For now, here are some high-level thoughts.

Project Content

"Content" is a term used to collectively refer to the types of information that appears on a webpage such as text, images, video, and audio. You've already read about what content displays on your project Home page in the "Anatomy Of A Kickstarter Project" section.

There are also some optional types of content you can add to your project Home page. For example, a video isn't required to launch a project, but most people consider it a really good idea to have one. Also, pledge graphics that show backers visual representations of the rewards for each pledge level can help your backers decided at which pledge level to support your project.

Creating content for your project Home page takes time and that time needs to be accounted for in your timeline.

Some things to consider:

- Who is writing the text?
- Who is creating the graphics?
- Who is shooting and editing the video?

If someone other than yourself is doing any of the above tasks, be sure to add time to review their work and for them to correct anything you want changed. There may need to be more than one cycle of review-and-change, so account for that as well.

This is where Work vs. Duration becomes very important. It may only take three hours of Work to write the text for your project Home page, but if you only have one hour a day due to other obligations, that's a Duration of 3 days, not 1 day of three hours, that needs to go into your timeline.

Account Information

Your account information needs to be filled out and verified before you can launch your project.

I'm mentioning it here because while most of the account information can be set up quickly, there is one aspect that is beyond your control, which is having your bank account verified. This can take anywhere from four business days to around two weeks, depending what happens on the bank's end.

2. Get Feedback And Prepare For Launch

Once your project content is done, put down this timeline date to get feedback and set up your project for launch.

Get Feedback

Since you created everything on your project Home page, it's a good idea to get someone else to take a look at it before you launch. You can create a Preview of your project Home page to share with a few people to get their feedback. They can check for typos, clarity, and an overall review of how you've presented your idea. Whether you act on this feedback is entirely up to you.

You can also submit your project for review by a Kickstarter Community Manager. Each Community Manager is a specialist in their category and often a creator themselves.

Prepare For Launch

Prior to June 2014, every project had to be reviewed by Kickstarter before going live. Now, your project could qualify for their Launch Now feature which uses an "algorithm incorporating thousands of data points to check whether a project is ready to launch—things like the project's description, rewards, funding goal, and whether the creator has previously launched a project."

If your project qualifies, you can launch at any time. If not, you have to submit your project for review by Kickstarter. Just in case that happens, allow a few extra days between the date you submit your project for review and when you want to launch it.

Once your project passes review, you can launch immediately or wait until a specific date.

3. Campaign Launches

This is the day your project goes live on the Kickstarter website and people can start pledging money to help you reach your funding goal.

If your project launch has to happen on a certain day, be sure you have enough previous days in your timeline to get everything done as mentioned above. Also be sure to allow enough time in case of a Kickstarter review as well as a few more days if you need to change something and resubmit for another review.

Once your project has launched, it'd be a really good idea to post updates about your project's progress. You don't have to account for these updates in your timeline, but a note as a reminder might be helpful.

4. Campaign Ends

The campaign for a project can last from 1-60 days. According to the Kickstarter website, the projects with the highest success rates run 30 days.

Shorter than thirty days and you have less time for people to find and pledge to your project.

Longer than thirty days and it can be difficult to keep up excitement for the project. Longer campaigns also push the estimated delivery date of rewards even further out. That said, longer campaigns have more time to get the word out and achieve stretch goals.

If there is an important event that would help with promoting your project, you can shorten or extend your campaign by a few days around that 30 day recommendation.

Whatever campaign length you decide on, the day your project ends is an important one in your timeline. Because assuming your project meets its funding goal, this is when the real work begins.

5. Money Is In Your Bank Account

First, assuming your project funds, you should take a day off and celebrate because you have just leveled up. You also now have what can sometimes be the hardest part of the Kickstarter journey ahead of you.

Second, there is a 14 day period after your campaign ends during which money is collected from your backers. This means the money from your successful project can be withdrawn to your bank account two weeks after your project closes, which is why you should note this date in your timeline. If other people/companies need to be paid in order to create the rewards for your backers, you won't be able to do that right after your campaign ends because you won't have the money yet.

Also, until these 14 days are over, you don't really know how much money your project truly raised or how many backers are getting rewards. A pledge just means the backer intends to send the money. Due to the Kickstarter fixed-funding model, no money is taken from backers until the campaign ends and has met or exceeded its funding goal. Therefore, when it comes time to collect money from backers, not all of them may pay the amount they pledged. And if they didn't pay, you shouldn't ship them any rewards.

If there is an issue with collecting a payment, the backer will receive several emails during the week right after your campaign ends. These emails are sent automatically so you don't have to do anything. If the backer doesn't correct whatever the problem is, they will show up labeled as "Dropped" on your Backer Report page.

Ideally your project exceeds your funding goal. If not, and if some backers don't pay, the amount of money collected may actually be less than your funding goal. Hopefully this won't happen to you, but it is a possibility you need to be aware of and plan for.

Once the 14 days are over, money can be withdrawn from the payment processor to your bank account. Both the Kickstarter fee of 5% and the payment processing fee of 3-5% will have already been taken out, so this money is now all yours, other than taxes.

For U.S.-based projects, if you have a six-month history of receiving credit card payments via Amazon Payments, you can withdraw your money immediately—as in, as soon as the pledge money is collected from the backer and the fees are processed, although I'd not recommend it. If you wait until the 14 day collection period is over, you can withdraw the total amount and have a clear record of exactly how much money you received for your records and for tax purposes.

6. Rewards Are Finished

Depending where you rewards are produced, onsite or offsite, you may need to account for a few extra weeks in your timeline.

Rewards Produced Onsite

If you're producing the rewards yourself, then the date you estimate you'll complete the last reward is the date to note on your timeline. In determining this date, you have to account for both Work and Duration, and I highly recommend you use the Scotty Principle.

Rewards Produced Offsite

If your rewards are produced at an offsite location, for example a printer, then this date technically isn't when the rewards have finished production. Because the rewards are offsite, it'll take time to get them to you, so you need to account for that shipping time. When you have the rewards in hand and ready to package, that's the date to put in your timeline.

For example, if it takes six weeks to print the rewards, they won't be at your door at the end of the six weeks. Depending what kind of shipping method you paid for, it may take two weeks or longer, or a whole lot longer if the location is in a different country, to reach your door.

When you work with vendors, you should get a production time estimate along with your cost estimate. Use those estimates, plus any shipping time that may be necessary, to note your "Rewards Are Finished" date.

And remember that "stuff" happens.

Even though a delay by the vendor may be out of your control, you are the one responsible for getting the rewards to your backers.

There is also the chance that between the time your project funds and the time you're ready to send the money to the vendor, you may not want to work with that vendor any more. Have a second choice vendor in mind, so if something does happen with your first choice, you aren't starting from scratch to locate a replacement which could push the delivery of the rewards past your estimated delivery date.

A NOTE ABOUT STRETCH GOAL REWARDS: If your project over-funds, depending on your stretch goals, more rewards may need to be produced, which may take more time. Since you can't know whether or not that will happen when creating your timeline, make some notes about what extra rewards are related to your stretch goals and how long you estimate it'd take to produce them.

---

7. Send Backer Surveys

Once your project has successfully funded, you'll be able to send a survey to your backers to request the information necessary to fulfill their rewards. There are more details about how to create your surveys in the "Part 4: Fulfill Your Promises" section.

There are two questions to answer about your surveys when creating your timeline:

- When do you want to send the surveys?
- How much time will you give Backers to answer their surveys?

When To Send The Surveys?

The best way to answer this question is to compare your project end date with the date your rewards will be finished. If there's a short amount of time between those two dates, say less than three months, you could send out your surveys soon after your project ends.

If there is a longer amount of time between those two dates, you may want to wait until a few weeks before you're ready to ship. Backers may change addresses and it's easier on everyone if the shipping addresses backers send in their surveys are the right ones.

If a backer does move, they can change the address they sent on their survey via the Kickstarter website if you haven't locked the survey addresses against changes. Backers may also contact you via a Kickstarter message or leave a comment that they need to change their address.

The possible exception to sending the backer surveys later than earlier is if you need information, like T-shirt sizes, in order to produce rewards. You can only send the survey once, so it's best to ask for all of the information you need for fulfillment at that time, so all of the answers will be consolidated in the backer report spreadsheets.

How Much Time To Answer The Surveys?

Unless you have a very small number of backers, as in under 25, it's unlikely all of them will answer their surveys within the time period you allot for that task. I personally know of one backer who took almost a year to answer a project's survey. Give your backers more than three weeks to return their surveys and be ready for the fact that when you start shipping your rewards, it is very likely you'll have to follow up on some missing addresses.

8. Process Backer Report Spreadsheets

When a backer replies to their survey, the information they send is put into a spreadsheet by Kickstarter. You can download these spreadsheets, called backer reports, from the Kickstarter website. There is one spreadsheet for each pledge level. I go into more detail of what to do with these spreadsheets in the "Part 4: Fulfill Your Promises" section.

To cover this at a high level as it relates to your timeline, just know that you can use the backer report spreadsheets to create checklists and address labels. If you have a small number of rewards to ship, you could hand address the packages, although that can introduce a greater chance of error compared to printing the addresses.

The format of the backer report spreadsheets (file type .csv) isn't "print ready" for shipping labels or for checklists. This means you, or someone you know, will have to spend time getting the spreadsheets into a usable format for what you want to do. It'll also depend on how many backers you had. Processing spreadsheets for 100 backers takes a lot less time than for 800 backers.

If you have no idea how to estimate this, add a week.

9. Start Packing Rewards

This is the day you have all of your rewards in hand, all of the shipping and return labels and checklists are ready, and you can start putting rewards into their packaging. Packing your rewards may or may not take a long time depending on if you're sending your rewards digitally, physically, or both.

Digital Rewards

If your reward is digital, you need to get the file to your backers. This can be done by using a third-party service like Dropbox or Hightail (formerly YouSendIt), or by uploading the file to a server you have access to, such as where your website is hosted. Wherever you put the file, make sure that place can handle the number of backers who will be downloading it.

It's also a good idea to limit the amount of time that the file will be available, so if possible, set an expiration date on the link or take down the file after a certain amount of time has passed. If any backer contacts you that they didn't receive the file, you can put it up again and only send the link to those backers who specifically request it.

Physical Rewards

If your rewards are physical, think about every task you need to do for each reward to be ready to take to a shipping service. Some questions you'll want to answer are:

- Do any of the rewards have to be signed or personalized? If so, that adds time.
- Is the packaging ready to go, or does flattened cardboard need to be folded into a box and taped?
- Are you shipping more than one package to each address? If so, you'll need to print more than one shipping label for each backer. It'd also be a really good idea to have a checklist to make sure every reward goes to the correct place.

How Long To Pack Your Rewards?

I recommend doing a practice run of packing the rewards. Do the most complex order that's possible. Go through all of the motions, such as making a box, wrapping a reward, packing the box, sealing the box with tape, putting on the shipping label, putting on the return label, and noting which backer it is on the checklist.

Once you time yourself doing all of the tasks from start to finish, you have a rough idea of how long it'll take to pack the rewards for one backer in minutes. Multiply that time by your estimated number of backers for a successful project and divide by 60. Now you have how long the Work takes as hours.

If your project over-funds and you have more backers, there will be more Work, so add a bit of time in the hopes you have an overly successful project.

Now think about when, during an average week, you have time to pack rewards along with everything else you usually need to get done. How much time, realistically, can you devote to packing rewards each day?

Take the average number of hours you have per day to pack, and divide that into the Work hours needed—that is your Duration in days.

I want to give you an example because that Duration can get longer than you think. Say it takes you about 15 minutes to pack one reward, from start to finish. If you have 200 backers, that's 3000 minutes or 50 hours of Work. If you can spend two hours a day packing, that's 25 days of Duration—almost a month just to pack the rewards. Now imagine if you had more than 200 backers ...

Also consider if there are people who could help you pack who would do a good job. Remember, if a backer gets the wrong rewards, they'll complain to you, not the person who packed the box.

If there are some folks you can rely on, you may be able to shorten the Duration needed to pack all of the rewards. Be sure to add a bit of buffer time for instructions and answering questions and setting up a work area to accommodate everyone.

Whether you work on your own or in a group, remember it's better to take extra time during packing to get everything correct than to have to deal with shipping out replacements.

If you're shipping rewards internationally, you'll probably also need some time to fill out customs forms.

Now that you have an estimate for how long it will take to pack your rewards, make a guess as to how long it will take to ship them.

- Will you print prepaid postage labels at home and drop off the packages at a shipping service?
- Do you need to take in one of the final packages as an example, buy all the postage, and then come home and put it on all of the boxes?
- Will you take all of the boxes to the shipping facility for them to put postage on each package, one at a time?

Regardless of how you do it, getting the rewards out of your house and on their way to your backers will take a bit of time you should account for in your timeline.

10. Estimated Delivery Date

One of the required pieces of information you have to fill out when you create a pledge level is the estimated delivery date. You need a month and a year, and those can be different for each pledge level if that's appropriate for your project.

The estimated delivery date is when you promise to deliver the rewards to your backers. As far as your backers are concerned, it's the most important date in your timeline because it sets their expectations of when they'll receive their rewards. And they can get very vocal if that date goes by and their rewards aren't in their hands.

People know unexpected things can happen to delay a project. The best way to deal with that is to let your backers know what's going on as soon as you do. Keeping people in the loop does wonders for maintaining a good relationship. Keep communicating and you have a much better chance of gaining your backers' understanding and patience.

The estimated delivery date should take into account how long it takes for your backers to receive their rewards. This means when they get the packages in their hands, not when you leave the packages at the shipping service.

If you're shipping via the cheapest method possible, packages will take some time to reach their destinations. For example, Media Mail by the U.S. Post Office can take up to two weeks or longer to deliver nationally, so if you plan to use that shipping method in the middle of the month, use the Scotty Principle and set your estimated delivery date to the following month.

Also consider that international mail will likely take longer to deliver than domestic mail. If a backer gets their rewards earlier than the estimated delivery date, you probably won't hear about it. If a backer gets their rewards later than the estimated delivery date, you'll definitely hear about it—so make sure that date is far enough out to account for international backers.

A Note About Christmas: If folks need their rewards in time for Christmas, plan to ship by late

October to give the national and international orders time to get to their destinations. There's also time for backers to ship off the rewards again if they're gifts. And if any orders are returned, you have a chance of contacting the backer and sending the box out again so it might still make it under the tree in time.

Part 2: Create Your Project

Having done all the work to define your project, determine your funding goal, define your pledge levels, create your timeline, and review exactly what kind of content goes where on your project Home page, you are ready to create your project on the Kickstarter website.

Creating a project on Kickstarter involves using a set of webpages that let you enter your project Home page content, your financial information, and your profile information. There's a way to preview your project Home page, and even send that preview to other people, without your project going live to the entire Internet. The last step, after you've completely filled out all of the necessary content and information, is to launch your project.

To begin the process, you need to sign up for a Kickstarter account.

Sign Up

If you haven't already done so, create a Kickstarter account by clicking on the "Sign up" link in the top-right corner (http://www.kickstarter.com/signup).

It's a simple process that requires your email address and a password, or you can use your Facebook login credentials. I've got a few notes about the Facebook connect option in the "Before You Start" section.

Once you have your Kickstarter account, log in by clicking on the "Log in" link also at the top-right corner (http://www.kickstarter.com/login).

Start A Project

After you've logged into your Kickstarter account, click on the "Start" link in the top navigation to go to the Start a Project page.

This page will give you an overview of the Kickstarter process and go into a few details such as fees. There are also several useful links under the "Help" heading in the Kickstarter footer.

When you're ready, click the "Start a Project" button.

You'll be asked to choose a category for your project and give it a title. Both of these options can be changed later. You can set which country you're in via the link under the "Continue" button. As of mid-June 2014, you can create a Kickstarter project if you live in the United States, the United Kingdom, Canada, Australia, New Zealand, and the Netherlands. When you're ready, click the "Continue" button.

Congratulations, you've just created a Kickstarter project! You'll also receive an email from Kickstarter that has links to tips, best practices, and their Help Center.

Project Tabs

Now that you've created a project, you need to provide the content and information for that project. You do this on pages accessed via the Project Tabs.

A NOTE ABOUT ACCESSING THE PROJECT TABS: If you've just created your project, after you set your category, title, and click on the "Continue" button, you end up on the Basics Project Tab.

If you've already created your project and are coming back to it at a later time, you first need to log into your Kickstarter account. Then click on your profile picture in the top-right corner. On the overlay that displays, click on the title of your project to go to the Basics Project Tab.

The Project Tabs display horizontally across the top of the pages under a simplified Kickstarter header.

Project Tabs with white checkmarks on a green circle indicate that as far as Kickstarter is concerned, you've completed all of the information required on that page. Project Tabs with white checkmarks on gray circles indicate you still need to provide content or information before your project can go live. The exceptions to this are the Preview Project Tab and the Continue Project Tab on the far right, which I'll cover later.

You can move from one Project Tab to another by clicking on them at the top of the page.

After you've entered or edited information on a Project Tab, a green "Save" button will appear as an overlay attached to the bottom of the browser window so no matter where you've scrolled to on the page, you can always get to it. Be sure to click that button or whatever work you did since the last time you saved will be lost if you leave that Project Tab. If you've made changes you don't want to keep, click the "Discard changes" link beside the "Save" button and the Project Tab will revert to its previous state.

If you want to review the Kickstarter rules, click on the "Our Rules" link in the top right beside your profile picture. This will take you to the Our Rules page which includes links to the prohibited items page, a page regarding prototypes and renderings, and the Community Guidelines page. To return to the Project Tabs, you can use your browser's Back button, or click on your profile picture to show an overlay that will let you click on your project title.

To leave the Project Tabs and return to the general Kickstarter pages, click the Kickstarter logo at the top left, or click on your profile picture at the top right to see the overlay of links to your account information and projects you have backed.

A NOTE ABOUT DELETING YOUR PROJECT: If you decide you want to delete your project, click the "Delete project" link which is located in the bottom right corner on all of the Project Tab pages. When you click on the "Delete project" link, your project won't immediately disappear. On the new page that displays, you need to enter your Kickstarter password and the phone number you used to verify your account. When you click the large red "Delete project" button, your project will be removed. If you don't want to delete your project, you can click on the "No, never mind" link and you'll be taken back to the Basics Project Tab.

Starting on the left, the Project Tabs are as follows:

- Basics
- Rewards
- Story
- About you
- Account
- Preview
- Continue

Basics

The Basics Project Tab requires content that I covered in the "Anatomy Of A Kickstarter Project" section. I'll do a quick recap here of the file format details you need to adhere to when providing this content.

Project Image

- Image size: at least 640 x 480 pixels or any size larger that's a 4:3 ratio
- File size: no larger than 50 MB
- File format: JPEG, PNG, GIF, BMP
- Can be changed during your campaign

Project Title

- Maximum number of characters: 60 (includes spaces)

Category

- Set via a dropdown list
- Required

Sub–category

- Set via a dropdown list
- Optional

Short Blurb

- Maximum number of characters: 135 (includes spaces)

Project Location

- Start typing to see Kickstarter suggestions
- Must choose from list of suggested locations
- Displays as city/state if in the U.S., city/country if outside the U.S.

Funding Duration

- Must be between 1-60 days
- Enter the number of days for the campaign to run or select the date and time the project will end
- Can't be changed once the project has launched

Funding Goal

- A whole amount in the currency of your country within the range of 1 to 99,999,999
- Can't be changed once the project has launched

The Basics Project Tab also has a preview of your project thumbnail which displays on the right side of the page. As you fill out information, the project thumbnail will also fill out so you can see what it will look like on the various Kickstarter pages that display project thumbnails, such as on the Discover page (http://www.kickstarter.com/discover).

Rewards

The Rewards Project Tab is the page where you enter the information about your pledge levels. The information you enter here will display in the right column on your project Home page.

Each pledge level is called a "Reward." You can have over 20 pledge levels, although too many can be confusing to your potential backers. Also keep in mind that you'll have to send a backer survey for each pledge level after your campaign ends.

To add a new pledge level, click the "Add another backer reward" link under the last pledge level on the page. You can add a new pledge level without filling out all of the information for a previous pledge level, however those empty pledge levels won't be saved. In order to save any pledge level, all of the required information must be filled in or it'll be highlighted in red when you click the "Save" button.

If you wish to change something about a pledge level once your campaign has started, you can only do so if no one has pledged to it. If a pledge level already has a backer, you can't change any of the information associated with it.

You can add new pledge levels at any time during your campaign.

For each pledge level, you have to fill out the following information:

Pledge Amount

- Must be whole dollars in the currency of your country
- Minimum: $1
- Maximum: $10,000 (different amount outside the U.S.)

Description

You want to keep this text as short and succinct as possible since it displays in a narrow column on the right side of your project Home page with an average of seven words per line.

You can put in a URL (EX: http://www.heidi2524.com), but it won't be clickable, so it's better to put your URLs in your project description where you can make them active links.

Estimated Delivery Date

- Month and year are set via dropdown lists
- Years available include the current year and five years out from that (EX: in 2014, the "Year" drop-down list includes years 2014 to 2019).
- Can be different for each pledge level

Shipping Details

This is set via a dropdown list with the following options:

- Shipping anywhere in the world
- Shipping within your country only
- No shipping involved

If you select "Shipping anywhere in the world," you have the option to add a fee for international backers in a whole dollar amount. This additional shipping fee is a suggestion and is not enforced by Kickstarter—a backer must add the additional shipping fee to their pledge on their own.

Limit Quantity

- By default, the checkbox is not selected
- Minimum: 1
- Maximum: 2,147,483,647
- Can be changed during the campaign

Selecting this checkbox limits the number of backers who can pledge to the value you entered. Once that number of pledges are made, the pledge level is marked as "All gone!" and no one else can support at that pledge level.

A NOTE ABOUT EDITING PLEDGE LEVELS: When you return to the Rewards Project Tab, all of the pledge levels will be in a collapsed state. In order to edit a pledge level, click on the pencil icon to the right of the pledge level amount. This expands that specific pledge level so you change the information.

Story

The Story Project Tab has four pieces of content that display on your project Home page. Two need to be completed before you launch your project, one is optional, and one can't be added until your project is live.

I covered more about this in the "Anatomy Of A Kickstarter Project" section and will recap any specifics you need here.

Project Video

- Optional, highly recommended
- File size: no larger than 5 GB
- File format: MOV, MPEG, AVI, MP4, 3GP, WMV, FLV
- Video encoding: WMV on Windows, H.264 on Mac
- Dimensions: 640 x 480 or larger, 4:3 ratio (if using a smartphone, be sure the width is longer than the height/uses a landscape format—you may have to rotate your phone 90 degrees)
- Can be changed during your campaign

The quality and size of your video depends on the bit rate. If your video program uses kbps (kilobits per second), start with 1,500. If your video program uses Mbps (megabits per second), set that to 1.5. Raise or lower the bit rate depending how the quality and size of your video turns out when you render it to one of the above file formats. A larger bit rate will have a larger file size and better quality. A lower bit rate will have a smaller file size but less quality.

Project Description

- Required
- Can include text, images, video and audio files
- Can be changed during your campaign

Use the formatting buttons above the description text box to make part of your text bold or italic, create a list, or increase the size of the selected text to that of a heading. Click on the appropriate button to make a URL an active link or to remove a link. You'll also use these buttons to add a video file, audio file, or image.

Risks And Challenges

- Required
- Text only

Project FAQ

- Optional
- Added after project is live
- Consists of question and related answer

About You

The About You Project Tab shows some of the same information that's also in your Profile. If you've already filled in some of your Profile, that information will show up here. Likewise, if you change any of the connected information on the About You Project Tab, it will also change for your Profile.

Profile Picture

- Image size: 220x220 pixels or larger in a 1:1 ratio
- File size: no larger than 50 MB
- File format: JPEG, PNG, GIF, BMP
- Can be changed during your campaign

Name

- Once you launch a project, this can't be changed

Facebook Connect

- Allows use of Facebook login credentials for some tasks
- Can be connected or unconnected at any time

Biography

- Optional
- Place for you to tell a bit about yourself
- Can be changed during your campaign

Your Location

- Start typing to see Kickstarter suggestions
- Must choose from list of suggested locations
- Can be different from the project location
- Can be changed during your campaign
- Displays as city/state if in the U.S., city/country if outside the U.S.

Websites

- Type in a URL (Kickstarter adds "http://" if you don't)
- First URL displays on project Home page
- Additional URLs display on Profile overlay and on Profile page
- Can be changed during your campaign

Kickstarter doesn't do any error checking on what you type in as a website, so be sure to click on the links on the Preview of your project Home page to assure they go where they should.

If you decide you don't want to connect your Facebook account to your Kickstarter account, you can add your Facebook page as a website (EX: http://www.facebook.com/heidi2524).

A NOTE ABOUT THIS INFORMATION: If you have already launched a project on Kickstarter, this Project Tab will already be filled out for you based on what you previously entered. Everything will be editable except your name.

Account

There are three things you need to take care of on the Account Project Tab. Since I'm in the U.S., these will be U.S.-based examples. Different information, and a different process to verify that information, may be used in other countries.

The Account Project Tab is where you provide information for the payment processor. In the U.S., Kickstarter uses Amazon Payments. Other countries use different payment processors.

As soon as you know you're going to create a project, it's best to get this taken care of as the process can take 7-14 days to complete.

Amazon Payments

You need an Amazon Payments business account in order to process the credit card payments of your backers. Setting up that account happens on the Amazon.com website.

Your Amazon Payments account is different than your personal shopping account, so be sure to keep track of the login information you set up, especially if you make it different than your personal shopping account.

After you have set up your Amazon Payments account, you'll need to verify it, which can take up to seven days. Verification includes confirming your email address, your bank account information, having a valid credit card on file, and completing your tax profile. The Kickstarter website has a page that walks you through these tasks (http://www.kickstarter.com/help/amazon).

Depending where you live (urban or rural), who you bank with, and how you choose to verify your bank account, that process can take a few business days or up to two weeks.

That's why it's a good idea to take care of this payment processor information now so it doesn't hold up the launch of your project later.

If you've already launched a Kickstarter project, your identity and contact information will already be verified. You'll still need to link to your Amazon Payments account.

A NOTE ABOUT NON-PROFITS: U.S. non-profit organizations can run Kickstarter projects as long as it is a "project" meaning there are specific rewards that go to backers, and the project follows the other Kickstarter rules. Kickstarter can't be used as a general fundraiser. There are other online crowdfunding websites that are dedicated to that purpose.

You'll have to fill out additional information for your organization, such as your EIN and also prove your non-profit status by sending in a copy of your IRS letter that shows you are a 501C(3).

Identity Verification

In order to verify you are who you say you are, you need to fill in three things:

- Legal name, first and last
- Birthday via dropdowns for year, month, and day
- Street address, city, state, and zip code

Contact Details

Kickstarter needs to verify two ways to contact you:

- Email address
- Phone number

To verify your email address, you click a button and Kickstarter sends a verification email to the email address you entered. When you get that email, click on the link inside it and you'll be all set.

To verify your phone number, you can choose a text message or an automated phone call. I chose the automated phone call and it happened within a few minutes of clicking that option on the Kickstarter website.

Preview

The Preview Project Tab displays on the far right and is slightly set apart from the other Project Tabs. This is because clicking the Preview Project Tab will take you to an unpublished version of your project Home page.

When on the Preview page, directly under the Project Tabs is a black bar with a green link that says, "Get preview link." When you click that link, the text will go away and a URL will display in that black bar. The URL will start with "http://www.kickstarter.com/projects," then have a number (or your vanity URL if you've set one up in your Profile settings), and end with a string of numbers, the word "token," and a bunch more numbers. You can highlight and copy this link off the webpage and send it to people so they can give feedback on your project Home page before you launch.

If you created a Preview link, your project isn't live on the Kickstarter website. Only the people who have that long URL can see your project Home page, however there is nothing stopping anyone from seeing it either, as it doesn't required a login or password to access. Therefore, when you share your Preview link, it's a good idea to mention you don't want that URL spread around the Internet.

Send that Preview link to a few people and ask for their thoughts. Tell folks they can leave their feedback directly on the Preview webpage, but if they do, other people who go to the Preview will also be able to see what was written.

Since some folks might want to make their comments confidentially, let them know how they can contact you when you send them the Preview link.

Other people often see things you've missed. They may have ideas about how you could better represent what you're doing or they may have suggestions regarding your rewards. Listen to what they have to say and then decide whether or not you want to change anything. It's your project and you're the one who ultimately needs to be happy with it.

You can disable the Preview link at any time by clicking the "Disable preview link" link that's also in the black bar under the Preview Project Tab and to the right of the Preview link URL. Once disabled, if anyone goes to that URL, they'll no longer be able to see your project.

Continue

Once you've completed all of the required information on the other Project Tabs, and you've had a few people look at your Preview, click on the Continue Project Tab.

Your project will be automatically evaluated by Kickstarter's Launch Now feature, which takes into account the information you provided as well as whether or not this is your first project. If your project passes, you can launch whenever you want. You also have the option to submit your project to a Kickstarter Community Manager if you want their feedback and advice.

If your project doesn't qualify for the Launch Now feature, it will have to be reviewed by Kickstarter. Sometime in the next few days, you'll receive an email about whether or not your project has been approved. Once approved, you can start your campaign at any time.

If your project was rejected, the email should tell you why. After addressing that issue, you can submit your project for review by Kickstarter again.

Part 3: Run Your Campaign

Once you've launched your project, you have however many days you decided to run your campaign to meet your funding goal.

Having a project live on the Kickstarter website isn't like a field of dreams where "if you build it, they will come." You have to tell people, a lot of people, often several times, about your project in order to get backers to pledge their money. Your project needs daily and weekly attention from you in order to succeed.

There are four areas you should focus on while running your campaign:

- Promote like your project depends on it
- Maintain your project Home page
- Send updates
- Communicate with your backers

You also get access to a set of webpages that have Creator Tools to help you accomplish the above tasks such as a Dashboard, the ability to post updates, backer report spreadsheets, and the ability to send your backers a survey after the campaign ends.

A Note About Canceling Your Project: If things go so badly that getting the rewards to your backers is in serious jeopardy, you can cancel your project. Any pledges you have received will be voided, no one new can pledge to your project, and you and all of your backers will receive an email. You and your backers can still post comments since your project will remain on the Kickstarter website. Even if you delete your Kickstarter account, your project will still be viewable.

Creator Tools

The Creator Tools are pages on the Kickstarter website that provide different ways for you to follow the progress of your project, update the project Home page, communicate with backers, and then request information from your backers so you can send their rewards after the end of your campaign.

After you've logged into your Kickstarter account and clicked on your project title from the overlay options available under the thumbnail of your Profile picture at the top right, the Creator Tools show up on the left side on a black bar that runs the length of the page.

At the very top of the black bar is a link to the Kickstarter home page. Under that is a thumbnail of your project image, which will load your project Home page when clicked. Under the project image thumbnail are links to the Creator Tools. These links go to pages that are specific to your project:

- Edit project
- Post update
- Check dashboard
- View backer report
- View messages
- Manage surveys

At the bottom of the bar are links to pages on the Kickstarter website that aren't specific to your project: the Creator Handbook, the contact page for Kickstarter, the Creator FAQ, and a link to log out of your Kickstarter account.

A Note About The Kickstarter Header And Creator Tools: When you see the black bar and links to the Creator Tools on the left side of the page, you'll no longer see the Kickstarter header.

Click the vertical "Hide" button near the top right of the black bar, and the bar will collapse to the left, out of the way. The Kickstarter header will display again, so you can get to the other links related to your personal account, the projects you have backed and created, and your general messages.

On the left edge of the page under the Kickstarter header, the "Hide" button is now a "Show" button. When clicked, the black bar with the links to the Creator Tools will display again.

If you go to a page not related to your project, the black bar and "Show" tab will disappear, and you'll have to select your project from the overlay options available under the thumbnail of your Profile picture at the top right in order to access the Creator Tools again.

Edit Project

When you click this link, you'll be taken to the same Project Tabs you used to create your project.

Since your project is live, you'll no longer have a need for some of the Project Tabs such as Preview and Continue.

The other Project Tabs, like Basics, Rewards, and Story let you update parts of your project Home page such as the project image, video, and pledge levels.

As soon as you click the "Save" button at the bottom of whichever Project Tab you worked on, those changes are immediately applied to your project Home page for everyone to see. After making any changes, be sure to look at your project Home page to see that things turned out the way you intended.

If you need a refresher on the parts of a project Home page, go to the "Anatomy Of A Kickstarter Project" section. Details about the Project Tabs are found in the "Part 2: Create Your Project" section.

The "Edit project" link won't be available after your campaign ends.

Post Update

An update is like a blog post that displays on the Updates page of your project.

When you post an update, it's also emailed to all of your backers. Each update has the following characteristics:

- Number
- Title
- Body
- View setting

Number

Kickstarter will automatically number all of your updates starting at number one. It's a handy bit of information if you want to refer someone to a specific update as you can reference it by number and title.

Title

The purpose of the title of an update is to let people know what kind of information is in the body of the update. You have 255 characters, including spaces. Your title can be specific as in "Sending the surveys this week!" or vague and curiosity-inducing as in "Guess what happened today?"

Body

The body of your update is the information you're sending to your backers. You can include links, videos, images, and audio files. There are also some buttons that will let you format your text as bold or italic, as a list, or as a heading.

View Setting

You have two options for the "Who can view this post?" setting of your update:

- **Anyone**: the update can be viewed by anyone who goes to the Updates page of your project.
- **Backers**: the update will only display the number and the title on the Updates page of your project. If a backer has logged into their Kickstarter account, they can go to the Updates page and read the entire update. Anyone who isn't a backer, even if they're logged into their Kickstarter account, will only see the number and title of the update.

You can send an update to all of your backers, or only backers of one or more pledge levels.

Select which pledge levels you want to send the update to by clicking the "Select tiers" button. Your pledge levels will display, and you can select the checkboxes of the pledge levels whose backers you want to receive that update. If you move your cursor over the blue "i" icon on the right, you'll see the pledge description in a small overlay so you can verify you're sending the update to the correct backers.

Once you've written your update, click on the "Save & preview" link in the top-right corner. Kickstarter will show you a preview of how your update will display.

If it looks good, click the "Publish" button near the top of the page and the update will be sent as an email to your backers and posted to your Updates page. Even if you only select one pledge level of backers, the update will still show up on your Updates page.

If you want to change something, click on the "Edit" link to the left of the "Publish" link, and you'll go back to the Post Update page. Once you've completed your edits, click the "Save & preview" link to see the updated version.

After you publish an update, you can edit it for the next 30 minutes. To change something in a published update, go to that specific update on the Updates page and click on the "Edit" link that appears on the right, near the update title. You'll be back on the Post Update page and can make whatever changes you need and then publish the update again. Your changes will appear on the Updates page but another email isn't sent to your backers, so if you changed something significant that you need people to know about, publish a new update so they'll get an email about it.

You'll want to make most of your updates readable by anyone, as this also includes search engines. Backer-only updates can be things related to rewards, such as links for downloads or questions that only people who have pledged should be allowed to answer.

Check Dashboard

Your Dashboard has information about the funding status of your project, a way to keep you aware of backer comments, and some information that could help you promote your project. There are six sections to your Dashboard:

- Project activity
- Funding progress
- Referrers
- Project video stats
- Reward popularity
- Activity list

Project Activity

At the top of the Dashboard, you get a snapshot of how your project is doing at that moment in time:

- Project title
- Campaign launch date
- Campaign end date/deadline
- How much money has been pledged
- Percent the project is funded, which can become greater than 100%
- Number of backers
- Time left in the campaign measured as days, hours, minutes, or seconds depending on the amount of time left

After your campaign ends, the top-right corner will contain information about the payment processor. For U.S. creators, that'll be a link to your Amazon Payments account and your token. Your token is the reference number to use if you need to contact Amazon about any issues.

Funding Progress

This shows you a nice big graph plotting the (hopeful) increase in the amount of money pledged over the days of your campaign. Pledge money is listed on the left, the dates are along the bottom, and the percent funded is listed on the right.

The green line on the graph represents your funding goal and the dots represent individual days. If you move your cursor over a dot, an overlay will display exactly how much money was pledged, what percent your project had funded, and how many backers you had on that specific day.

Referrers

This area of the Dashboard can be really useful.

First, you have a pie chart that shows where your pledges come from—links on the Kickstarter website, or links outside the Kickstarter website (External).

To the right of the pie chart are the numbers—the amount pledged via Kickstarter links, the amount pledged from external links, and the average pledge amount.

Below the pie chart is a table that shows you the referrer, the type of referrer (Kickstarter or External), the number of pledges, the percent pledged, and the amount pledged via that referrer. If you click on one of those headings, the table will sort itself either alphabetically (A to Z) or numerically (smallest number at the top) based on what kind of information is in that column. Click on the same heading a second time and the sort order will reverse (Z to A, largest number at the top).

Sometimes a link shows up in the referrer column. If it has a small question mark icon beside it, you can mouse over that icon to see an explanation.

If you have a specific URL show up as a referrer, you can copy and paste that link into your browser and see if you can find out where your project was mentioned. If there's a way to post to that page, you could thank them, or if there are any questions on that page, you could answer them. You may also want to post an update with some referrer links which have other people talking positively about your project.

Project Video Stats

Here you'll see the total number of times your project video was played (on Kickstarter and externally) in big, black numbers, and under that, in small gray numbers, the percentage of video plays that were completed. As I mentioned earlier, don't stress about that. My Wish Cranes project video was only 48 seconds long and just over 25 percent of the people who started the video didn't finish it.

To the right of the Project Video Plays is a bar chart which shows you how many video plays came from the Kickstarter website compared to how many came from offsite. When someone uses the "Embed" link under the video on your project Home page to put your project video on their webpage, that's considered an offsite play.

Reward Popularity

This bar chart lets you know which of your pledge levels are the most popular. You can roll over any bar and get the following details for that reward:

- Pledge amount
- Number of backers
- What percent those backers are of your total number of backers
- Amount of money pledged
- What percent that money is of the total money pledged

As your campaign runs, these bars will grow as more backers select their pledge levels. If one or two pledge levels stand out as being very popular, you could specifically promote those pledge levels as they may be more likely to appeal to new people.

If you have any stretch goals tied to specific pledge levels, this bar chart will quickly tell you how many backers will be getting those stretch goal rewards.

Activity List

At the bottom of your Dashboard is the Activity list. This list provides information about what your backers are doing regarding pledges and comments and is always ordered with the most recent activity at the top of the list.

You can click on the backer's name to go to their Profile page. If you move your cursor over a row, the "Backer info" link will appear to the right and when clicked, displays the Backer Details overlay. I have more information about that in the *View Backer Report* chapter of the "Part 3: Run Your Campaign" section.

You can filter the Activity list in four ways:

- Everything
- Pledges
- Adjustments
- Comments

Everything

This is the default state of the Activity list which means you see all of the types of activities that are going on in your project: updates, pledges, adjustments, and comments. Each row displays the type of activity (EX: comment), the backer's name, their activity (EX: how much they adjusted their pledge) and the date.

Pledges

If you click on this link, the Activity list will only show you the pledges made to your project. Each row shows the backer's name, how much they pledged, which pledge level they selected, and the date of the pledge.

Adjustments

If you click on this link, the Activity list will change to show only the changes that backers have made to existing pledges. The change could be an increase, a decrease, a change to a different pledge level, or a cancellation. Each row will list the backer's name, what changes they made to their pledge, and the date.

Comments

If you click on this link, the Activity list will only show comments made by yourself or your backers, as only backers can comment on your updates or on your project's Comments page.

For each row, the backer's name, their comment, and the number of the update to which the comment was related, will display. Clicking on the update number will take you to that update. Comments without update numbers were made on the project's Comments page.

Whenever someone leaves a comment on one of your updates or on your project's Comments page, you'll get an email with the backer's name, the comment, and a link to the page the comment was left on.

As you run your campaign, changing the Activity list to Comments is a quick way to scan through all of the comments left on your project. You can directly answer backers' questions by replying with a comment yourself. If you think the answer is of interest to more than the person who asked it, you could write an update or and an entry to the FAQ on your project Home page.

Posting a comment just to thank backers who leave comments is a nice way to connect with the people who are supporting your project. It also shows potential backers that you're engaged and care about the folks involved.

View Backer Report

Your Backer Report page shows all of the backers of your project and will help you keep track of and communicate with these people while you run your campaign and through fulfillment.

Each row in the list of backers displays the backer's number, the backer's name (which may or may not be their real name, as that information isn't required by Kickstarter unless you create a project), their pledge amount, and the number of messages sent between you and that backer.

Clicking on a row in the list of backers will display a Backer Details overlay which shows the following information:

- Backer name
- Backer number
- Backer email address
- Pledge amount and date pledged (month, day, year)
- Reward selected: pledge level amount, pledge level description, and estimated delivery date
- Link to "Add note to self," which when clicked, displays a text box where you can type in whatever information you want. This text won't display to the backer and is for your use only.

- Message tab, which when clicked, shows all messages between you and a specific backer, as well as allows you to send a message directly to that backer. This is how you'd send a "thank you" message if you wished to do so.

A NOTE ABOUT BACKER NUMBERS: When someone pledges to your project, they are incrementally assigned a number starting with #1. If a backer cancels their pledge, their backer number isn't re-assigned. As an example, by the end of your campaign, there may not be a backer #27.

There are three things you can do on the Backer Report page:

- Export backer information
- Message backers
- Use the list of backers

Export Backer Information

At the top right is a link called "Export", which when clicked, will display an overlay that lets you download information about your backers (name, address, etc.) as a spreadsheet file. I cover a lot more about what you do with the backer report spreadsheets once your campaign is over in the "Part 4: Fulfill Your Promises" section.

Message Backers

Also at the top right of the Backer Report page is a "Message backers" link.

If you want to send a message to all of the backers of a specific pledge level, or to all backers who have specifically not chosen a reward, click this link.

You'll see an overlay with a dropdown list that lets you select one of your pledge levels. When you click the "Continue" button, the overlay will change to show a large text box where you type in the message to send to those backers. Click the "Send message" button to send the message to all the backers of that pledge level. Click the "Cancel" link to remove the overlay without sending the message. Backers will receive your message as an email and can also see it when they log into their Kickstarter account.

Use The List Of Backers

The list on the Backer Report page shows all of the backers of your project at the time you view it. When you first load the Backer Report page, up to 100 backers will display if that many have pledged. When you scroll toward the bottom of the page, more backers will load into the table until the complete list displays.

The total number of backers in the list displays on the top left. Once the payments have processed after the end of your campaign, that number may be different than the number of backers displayed on your project Home page. The project Home page's number of backers is the number of people who pledged. The Backer Report page's number of backers is the number of people whose payments actually went through. For my Wish Cranes project, I had 271 people pledge but only 263 payments went through successfully.

You can click on some of the column headings above the list of backers to sort the list. If you click the "#" heading, the list will sort in order of the backer's number. Clicking the "Backer" heading will sort the list alphabetically by the backer's first name. Clicking the "Pledge" heading will sort the list numerically by the amount the backer has pledged—which may or may not be the same as a pledge level amount since backers can give any amount of money and select any available pledge level that's equal to or less than their pledge amount.

There are several ways to cut down the number of names displayed to help you find a group of backers or a specific person:

- Rewards dropdown list
- Backers dropdown list
- Search box

Rewards Dropdown List

The Rewards dropdown sits on the left, above the list of backer names. By default, it shows "All rewards."

If you click on the "Rewards" dropdown list, you'll see each of your pledge levels as options, from smallest pledge amount at the top, to the largest pledge amount at the bottom. The very last option is "No reward" which refers to backers who pledged money to support your project and specifically said they didn't wish to receive a reward.

Selecting a specific pledge level from the "Rewards" dropdown list will alter the list of backer names to show only the people who have selected that pledge level. Just above the table on the left will be the number of backers for that pledge level, the pledge level (EX: $8 reward), and a link to an overlay that shows the pledge level description, the estimated delivery date, and whether or not you have sent the survey for that specific pledge level.

Backers Dropdown List

During your campaign, the "Backers" dropdown list only has a few options. All of the options on this dropdown list become available after the end of your campaign. Options include the default of "All backers," backers who have and haven't responded to the survey, backers with notes, dropped backers, and backers for whom you have and haven't selected the "Rewards sent?" checkbox.

Search Box

On the left side, near the top of the page, is a Search box.

You can search for a backer's name using complete words or partial words, such as "John" or "Jo" or "Smi" to find "John Smith."

Only the username, the part of an email address preceding the @ sign, is searchable. If you put in the precise username, for example "houndstooth" of "houndstooth@gmail.com", you'll only get a result if it matches the information Kickstarter has on file for a specific backer. If you only put in a partial username, such as "hound", you won't get a result, unless what you type in happens to match or partially match a backer's name or is an exact match for someone's username.

To clear your search terms and reset the Backer list to show all names, click the "X" inside the Search box to the left of the "Search" button and give the page a moment to reload.

A NOTE ABOUT SEARCHING FOR BACKERS BY NAME: Once you have replies to the backer surveys, your backer report spreadsheet will have two columns with name information. The "Backer Name" column is the backer's Kickstarter account name. The "Name" column contains what the backer supplied in the survey. When using the search on the Kickstarter website, you need to look for the "Backer Name" as the survey answers aren't searchable.

For example, if a person's "Backer Name" is Bob and the name they put into the survey is "Robert Brown", search for "Bob" to find that specific backer. If you search for "Robert," you may get other backers whose account name contains "Robert," but it won't be backer "Bob."

View Messages

Clicking the "View messages" link displays a list of messages related to your project. Someone doesn't have to be a backer of your project to send you a message, they just need to have a Kickstarter account and have clicked the "Contact me" link on your project page.

Individual messages related to the same person are grouped together. What you see on the Messages page is a list of conversations. The conversation with the most recent message is listed at the top.

Each row shows a conversation with a different person and includes that person's Profile thumbnail, their name, the name of the project, and the first part of the most recent message. On the right of each row is the date of the latest message and the number of messages in that conversation.

Clicking on a row will display the messages in that specific conversation on the right side of the page. The left side of the page will continue to show the list of all conversations.

For each message in a conversation (when it displays on the right side of the page), you'll see both the person's messages to you and your messages to them. Each message has the Profile thumbnail, the name of the person sending the message, the date the message was sent, and the text of the message. Messages are ordered with the most current at the bottom. At the very bottom of the conversation is a text box where you can reply to the person with a new message. Clicking on their name will take you to their Profile page.

If you feel a message isn't appropriate, you can report it as spam by clicking the "Report Spam" link on the right, aligned with the person's name, when looking at a specific message in a conversation.

You'll also receive copies of messages via email. It's a good idea to check the Messages page as well, just to make sure you don't miss any questions from someone.

Send Survey

Once your campaign is over, and if your project reached its funding goal, you'll be able to send a survey to your backers to ask for the information you need in order to send their rewards. Depending on what the rewards are, you may need a physical address, an email address, a T-shirt size, etc.

Each pledge level has its own survey. So even if you need the same information from all of your backers, you'll have to set up and send a survey for each pledge level via the Kickstarter website—assuming you want Kickstarter to collect the backer information for you.

You don't have to use Kickstarter to send the surveys. I've pledged to two projects that ended up having thousands of backers. They chose to use their own websites and systems to collect backer information.

You do have to somehow get whatever information you need from your backers in order to fulfill your promises and send their rewards.

If you decide to use the Kickstarter surveys, I have more details about how to do so in the "Part 4: Fulfill Your Promises" section.

Promote Like Your Project Depends On It

The point of promotion is to connect with people who might be interested in helping your project be a success by pledging their money to your creation.

Ideally you've told people about your project before you launched it. Now that your project is live, you need to make some kind of effort to promote your project online and possibly offline as well.

I don't have any absolute must-do promotion techniques to tell you for two reasons. One, you don't technically have to promote your project. You may not reach your funding goal if you don't do any kind of promotion and the assumption is you do want to meet your funding goal. Two, a promotion technique that might work brilliantly for one project may do nothing for another.

The only advice I have is that you need to promote your project to someone or there won't be anyone to pledge to your funding goal.

Maintain Your Project Home Page

While the majority of your project Home page will stay the same during your campaign, you do have the ability to make some changes:

- Project description
- Project image
- Project video
- Pledge levels that don't have any backers
- Addition of new pledge levels
- Your profile bio

Project Description

Your project description should always contain the basic information about your project because (hopefully) new people are looking at your project Home page every day.

You should be posting updates about your project, which is where most of the new information will go. If you do make changes to your project description, the changes should enhance the basic information that's already there, not remove anything unless it's something you're no longer going to do for your project.

If the information is important enough for new people to see, you can put it at the top of the project description on your project Home page. Be careful about piling too much information here as you still want potential backers to be able to see what your project is about without having to scroll down through content that doesn't matter to them if they don't understand the project.

Here are some examples of information you may want to add or change in your project description during your campaign:

- Links to third-party sources who speak favorably about your project
- Mention if your project becomes a Staff Pick on the Kickstarter website
- Text or images about new pledge levels
- Stretch goals reached
- New add-ons

Project Image

Since your project image also displays in your project thumbnail, which shows up in a few places on the Kickstarter website, it's a good idea to keep it the same for most of your campaign. Changing it frequently could lose some potential backers if they go looking for a specific image and don't find it.

That said, as your project gets closer to its last day, you could update your project image to include large text regarding how many days are left.

Project Video

There are the same considerations for your project video as for your project description—if you change it, don't loose any information. Remember, once you do change the file, people visiting your project Home page won't have any reference to what your project video used to be or the information it used to have.

Pledge Levels That Don't Have Any Backers

If a pledge level doesn't have any backers, you can change it or remove it. If you do either of those things, it'd be a good idea to post an update about why you did so. You have no idea what backers will notice about your project and a change to something significant such as a pledge level should be explained.

If someone has already selected a pledge level, no aspect of that pledge level can be changed—unless that backer changes to a different pledge level or cancels their pledge.

Addition Of New Pledge Levels

As your campaign goes along, you may get ideas or suggestions for new pledge levels, or you may have planned to add a new pledge level as certain limited quantity pledge levels sell out. You can add a pledge level at any time during your campaign. If you do, as with changes to existing pledge levels, it's a good idea to post an update to tell your backers.

During my Wish Cranes campaign, I had several people ask for pledge levels where they could get more origami cranes than at the pledge levels I initially had when I launched my project. I created new pledge levels six days into my campaign, and again at 15 days into my campaign, and posted updates both times (http://www.kickstarter.com/projects/heidi2524/1000-origami-wish-cranes/posts/515038, http://www.kickstarter.com/projects/heidi2524/1000-origami-wish-cranes/posts/524143).

Your Profile Bio

If something spectacular happens to you that's worth putting in your Kickstarter Profile bio, you can change that text during your campaign. Depending on what the addition is, it may be worthy of an update.

Add A FAQ

The purpose of a FAQ (Frequently Asked Questions) is to cover things that aren't already explained on your project Home page. You can only add a FAQ to your project Home page after your project has launched and is live on the Kickstarter website. The FAQ is optional.

If you want to have a FAQ, you can add entries at any time during your campaign. To add a FAQ, log into your Kickstarter account and select your project from the overlay options you see when you click on your Profile thumbnail in the top-right corner of the page. Then click the "Edit project" link in the list of Creator Tools on the left side of the page.

You'll now be back in the Project Tabs.

Click on the Story Project Tab, and scroll to the bottom of the page. Here is where you enter the questions and answers that will become your FAQ. When you're finished entering the text, click the "Save" button at the bottom of the page. Whatever you wrote will now appear on your project Home page.

As you run your campaign, you may get questions from people about certain details of your project. You can always answer the person's question directly via a comment or a message, but adding your answer as a FAQ to your project Home page assures the information is easily available to everyone.

Check out other projects (from any category) and see if they have a FAQ on their project Home page and what kind of questions and answers they provide.

Also pay attention to the writing style and tone of the FAQs on other projects. Since a FAQ is part of your project Home page, you can extend whatever style you've used to write your project description (serious, humorous, etc.) as long as the answer to the question is clear and doesn't cause additional confusion.

A Note About Changing Your Project Home Page: Remember that whatever your project Home page looks like when your campaign ends, that's how it will look forever more. You can't change anything on your project Home page after time runs out on your funding period, no matter if your project is successful or not.

Communicate with Backers

As you run your campaign, it's important to keep in touch with people who engage with you and your project. These people could be backers or someone who has a Kickstarter account but hasn't yet pledged to your project. In order for someone to comment on your project's Comments page or on an Update, or send you a message via the "Contact me" link on your project Home page, they must use their Kickstarter account or have logged into the Kickstarter website using their Facebook credentials.

Your communications can be one-to-many or one-to-one, depending which method you use. Here are four ways you can keep in touch with people about your project:

- Post updates (one-to-many, backers-only, or anyone who comes to your project)
- Send "thank you" messages (one-to-one)
- Respond to comments (one-to-many)
- Respond to messages (one-to-one)

Post Updates

As you run your campaign, post updates. Let people know what's going on with you and your project. Other than your project Home page, updates are the most visible way to share yourself and your project with people in order to gain their financial support.

You decide if the update can be read by anyone who comes to your project or if an update should only be seen by your backers.

All updates are created on the Post Update page which I reviewed earlier in this section.

Updates can be about any number of things. Here are a few thoughts:

- Progress report (EX: just passed 25% funding)
- Extra information (EX: video interview)
- New information (EX: pledge level based on backer feedback)
- Reward information (EX: link to download a PDF, would want to make this a backer-only update)
- Promotion by other people (EX: link to third-party website that gave your project some good press)
- Appreciation (EX: how much you appreciate your backers' helping you achieve your dream)
- Delays (EX: printed rewards will take another two weeks than originally estimated)

You could create the content for some updates before you even launch your project. If you're co-creating a project, record some video interviews with the folks involved. Take photos of what you've done to this point on your project. Have behind-the-scenes photos of you creating your Kickstarter video if there's something special/fun/interesting about it. By having this kind of content already available, you don't have to worry about creating it while your campaign is running and it makes posting an update quicker and easier.

Updates don't have to be thousand-word essays. A few sentences and a photo or video are enough. You're providing additional value to your backers as well as keeping your project in their awareness.

In your updates, it's okay to ask your backers to help spread the word about your project. Some creators have a difficult time with self-promotion, but in this case, you've a certain amount of permission to ask for help because your backers have already pledged money to your project. It's in their best interest that your project funds so they can get their rewards.

As to how often you should post updates, that's entirely up to you. I recommend at least every ten days, more if there's a lot of activity going on related to your project.

Check out other Kickstarter projects to see how often they posted updates and what was in those updates. Also be sure to glance through the comments to see how the update was received by the backers.

It seems like an obvious thing, posting updates, however I've seen projects that didn't post any updates, or only had one update near the end of the campaign. Sometimes the project was successful, often it wasn't.

Send "Thank You" Messages

Once someone has backed your project, you can easily send them a message via the Kickstarter website. They'll receive the message as an email (if they have that setting of their Kickstarter account set up to do so) and they can read your message when they log into their account on the Kickstarter website.

Sending "thank you" messages are optional. I highly recommend you do so as every backer is taking a chance with their money on you and your project.

Your message can be as simple as "Thank you for backing my Kickstarter project, [name of your project]" and add your name. It's a nice bit of personal acknowledgment for the money the backer is giving in support of your project. Some backers may respond, most probably won't.

If you do decide to send "thank you" messages, don't feel obligated to do so right after a backer pledges. Pick a time each day and send the message to the new backers who have pledged since you last sent "thank you" messages.

Since the Backer Report page shows how many messages have happened with a specific individual, I'd only send the "thank you" messages to those new backers who didn't have any numbers listed in the Messages column. If a backer had already sent me a message first, I'd reply to that message and include my gratitude in that communication instead of sending a separate "thank you" message.

For my Wish Cranes project, I'd go to my Backer Report page each evening and send each new backer a "thank you" message. Most people didn't reply, a few did. I had some nice conversations with those few folks, and it was fun to learn more about my backers as they learned more about me.

Respond To Comments

Only backers can leave comments on your project, however these comments (and any comments you make) are visible to everyone.

There are two places on your project that backers can leave comments:

1. On the Comments page
2. On an update

By default, you'll receive an email whenever a backer leaves a comment, no matter where they post it on your project. You can opt out of getting such emails by clicking on the link at the bottom of a "New comment!" email, or going to the Edit settings page and clicking on the Notifications tab.

You can also see all of the comments that have been left on your project, no matter where they were posted, by going to your Dashboard, scrolling to the bottom of the page, and clicking the "Comments" link to filter your Activity List. I found this to be the easiest way to keep aware of comments while running my Wish Cranes project.

You don't have to respond to every comment, however if a backer asks a question, it's a really good idea to answer them in a timely manner.

If you won't have an answer for a while (more than a week), put that in your comment. People appreciate knowing what's going on. Most would rather see a comment of "the answer is coming" than be left wondering with no answer at all.

You can also post a comment just to engage with your backers and express your appreciation. If you're responding to a specific backer, use their name in your comment so they, and other people who read the comments, can see who you're addressing.

Respond To Messages

I recommend checking your project messages every 1-2 days while running your campaign.

To read messages that are related to your project, compared to messages you receive from the creators of projects you've backed, select your project from the overlay options that show when you click on the thumbnail of your Profile picture at the top-right corner of the page.

Now the black bar displays on the left side of the page, and you can click the "View messages" link in the list of Creator Tools links under the thumbnail of your project image.

Since a message can come from someone who hasn't pledged to your project, when and how you respond to their message may make up their mind whether or not they want to become a backer.

For any questions you get via a message, go ahead and answer the question as a message, and also consider if that question and answer should be a FAQ entry.

You may also receive messages that have nothing to do with your project. I've gotten messages from people promoting their own Kickstarter projects and from others who wanted to sell me a way to advertise my project. It's up to you how you respond to such messages, or if you respond at all.

If you feel a message is inappropriate, you can click the "Report spam" link that displays to the right of the sender's name.

Part 4: Fulfill Your Promises

If you've met your funding goal by the end of your campaign, your project is a success and you should celebrate! You should also realize you have an entirely new journey of challenges ahead of you.

Since your project funded, you are obligated to fulfill the promises you made of what rewards you'd send to your backers. If you don't fulfill those obligations in a timely manner, there could be legal consequences.

Because each Kickstarter project is unique, I can't give you specific details on how to create your rewards. I can go over at a high level the steps you should go through to fulfill your promises to your backers.

- Receive money
- Create rewards
- Send surveys
- Keep communicating
- Use backer report spreadsheets
- Ship rewards

A Note About Missed Backers: You may get a few messages after your campaign has finished from folks who wanted to be backers but didn't make it in time. It's up to you how you want to deal with them.

Whatever arrangement you make with people who want rewards after the campaign has ended, their information won't be in the backer report spreadsheets. You'll need to keep track of how much they pay, what rewards they'll receive, and have a way to get the information you need in order to fulfill their order, such as email address, mailing address, etc.

Receive Money

Most of what happens after the end of the campaign is entirely up to you to get done, with the exception of collecting the backers' pledge money.

For two weeks after the end of your campaign, the payment processor will try and retrieve the pledge money from your backers.

If there is an issue with a payment, the backer will receive an email and have a certain number of days to correct the problem. If they don't, the money isn't collected, so the amount of money you actually receive could be less than the amount listed as pledged on your project Home page.

During these two weeks, you can see the status of each backer's pledge on your Backer Report page which is accessed via the Creator Tools. A red icon will appear next to backers whose payments have issues. If you see any red icons after seven days, you can post an update reminding your backers to take care of any payment processing issues, or they will be dropped from the project and not receive their rewards.

Ideally, all of your backers end up with a status of "collected." Some may end up having a status of "dropped" which means their payment did not go through. To see all of the backers whose payments did not go through, click on the "Backers" dropdown list and select "Dropped backers."

Now that you know who they are, you can send a message to say their payment didn't go through, and therefore they won't receive their rewards. I know some creators who have done this. I didn't do it for my Wish Cranes project. It's totally up to you if you want to follow up with dropped backers or not.

Depending how the payment processor for your country handles things, the money may end up in the payment account (Amazon Payments for the U.S.), or go into the bank account you set up to receive the money. If you're in the U.S., the Kickstarter fees and the payment processor fees will be taken out for each transaction, so the money you receive into your Amazon Payments account is the final amount from your project. You'll likely have to withdraw the money from the Amazon Payments account into a bank account so you can use it to complete your project and create the rewards for your backers.

Once you know how much money you actually collected from your Kickstarter funding endeavor, set aside a chunk for taxes.

Now get ready to spend some money and get stuff done.

Create Rewards

Once you have the money in hand, use it wisely. Do what you said you were going to do on your project Home page to complete your project and produce the rewards.

Post updates as you go, along with pictures and/or video if possible. Post-campaign updates don't need to be weekly, but they should be there to show progress and reassure your backers you're using their money as they intended—to create something unique and to produce the rewards they pledged to receive.

Review the timeline you created to keep track of important dates and measure your actual progress against those estimates. If some hijinks happen that cause delays, do your best to keep your backers informed, especially if you're going to miss your estimated delivery date.

Send Surveys

Kickstarter has a way for you to send a survey to backers of each pledge level of your project. Using this survey is optional, however you'll need some way to get information from your backers and this is a simple way to do so.

I wrote up some thoughts about when to send your survey in the *Create A Timeline* chapter in the "Part 1: Define Your Project" section. Basically whenever you send the surveys, make sure there's enough time afterward for the backers to respond, for you to do what you need to do with those responses (EX: order t-shirts, create shipping labels, check-lists, etc.), and for the rewards to ship before hitting your estimated delivery date.

Once you send the survey, your backers will receive an email with a link to the survey, and they'll see a banner alerting them about the survey when they log into their Kickstarter account. They'll get a few reminders for the next two weeks. You'll also want to post an update reminding people to fill out their surveys and may even have to follow up with some people individually in order to get their answers. Out of 263 backers, I still had a few who didn't respond to their survey for several months after my Wish Cranes campaign ended.

What Information To Collect

Be aware that a survey can only be sent once to each pledge level, so spend some time crafting your surveys to try and make sure you ask for all of the information you need to send the rewards.

For physical rewards, at minimum, you need to know their mailing address. Depending on the reward, you may also need other information, such as size for clothing, preference if a selection of rewards is offered, etc.

For digital rewards, you can ask them for their email address, as they may want their reward sent to a different account than the one they used for Kickstarter.

If you had any add-on/a la carte rewards, add questions to your survey to have your backers tell you which ones they paid for in addition to their pledge level amount. It's important to get add-on information from your backers as there is no record of what the backer intended if they sent more money than the pledge level required.

If you find you need some information from your backers after you've sent the survey, you can post a backer-only update. The update can be to all backers or to a specific pledge level.

Another option is to send a message via the "Message backers" link in the top-right corner of the Backer Report page. A message can only be sent to one pledge level at a time, so you may have to send multiple messages if you want to reach backers in more than one pledge level.

Whichever method you use, be sure to also let your backers know how they should get their information to you, as in giving them an email address to use or ask them to reply via a Kickstarter message. Since comments can be read by anyone, that's not a recommended way to send personal information such as a mailing address.

Since your request wasn't part of the survey, the backers' answers won't be included in the backer report spreadsheets, so be sure to keep up with everyone's replies so you can fulfill their rewards correctly.

Create The Survey

The survey for each pledge level can be the same or different. This flexibility is great in that you don't have to ask questions of backers that don't apply to them. This also means you have to create as many surveys as you have pledge levels.

To create your surveys, click on the "Manage surveys" link in the list of Creator Tools on the left side of the page.

The Surveys page will have a list of all of your pledge levels and include the pledge amount, the number of backers, the estimated delivery date, the pledge description, and a "Create a survey" button.

Click on the "Create a survey" button for a specific pledge level to create that survey. On the Create survey page, the pledge level information will be shown at the top of the page. The left side of the page is where you'll edit your survey, and the right side of the page will show you a preview of the survey as you add each question.

The first thing you can do is add an introduction to the beginning of the survey. By default, you'll see the text "[your name] needs some info from you to deliver your reward." You can leave that text as is, or click into the text box and type in your own message.

Under the introduction text box is a gray box with the heading "Name & address." By default, the checkbox isn't selected. If you select the checkbox, a backer can change their address after they've answered the survey. It's a good idea to select that checkbox to make it easier on yourself regarding backer address changes.

When you get close to shipping your rewards, you can come back to the survey and "close" it—this means the backers will no longer be able to edit their addresses. When you close a survey, Kickstarter will send an email to the backers of that pledge level that they have 48 hours in which to change their address. Once address changes are no longer allowed, whatever address the backer put into the survey is the address that will show up in your backer report spreadsheets. If a backer needs to change their address after the survey has closed, they'll need to contact you and you'll have to keep up with their new address outside of the Kickstarter system.

In the preview of the survey on the right side of the page, you can see that Kickstarter has already put in text fields and dropdown lists for the backer's name and mailing address.

If you need to, you can add additional survey questions. Click the "Add question" button to add a text box question where the backer can type in their answer. Click the "Add multiple choice" button to add a multiple choice question for which you'll define all of the answers and the backer has to select one of them.

Multiple-choice questions are the easiest to work with because the answers you get back will have been selected from the choices you provided. Text box answers may require some interpretation since the backer can type in whatever they want, but they're the one to use when you need information that's unique to the backer, such as a name for a personalized reward.

If you ask a question on a survey, the backer has to answer it or the survey can't be submitted. If you have a multiple choice question that may not apply to some of your backers, make the last choice "None." If you have a text box question that some of your backers may not have to answer, be sure to add some kind of language to tell backers what to put if the question doesn't apply to them (EX: "Please list which add-ons you included with your pledge. If you didn't have any add-ons, put 'None'"). If you don't add that extra bit of instruction to explain that an answer needs to be given, some backers can get annoyed that they have to type in something instead of being able to leave it blank, even though requiring an answer for every question is determined by Kickstarter, not you—trust me on this one, some people get very annoyed.

When you're finished creating your survey, take a good look at the preview. Are you asking for all of the information you need? Are there any typos? Are the instructions on how to answer the questions as clear and complete as possible?

If you want to get rid of the survey and start from scratch, click the "Cancel" link. If you want to go away and come back to work on the survey later, click the "Save" button. If you're ready to send the survey, click the "Send survey" button. Backers of that pledge level will receive an email with a link to the Kickstarter website where they'll need to log into their account to answer the survey.

Now you get to create the survey for your next pledge level.

A Note About Backer Name And Email Address: It's a good idea to ask for the name and/or email address for a specific type of reward, such as a personalization or to receive an electronic reward. You shouldn't assume that information is the same as what Kickstarter has on file. A backer may want the option to send a reward as a gift in which case their Kickstarter account information isn't what you need to fulfill the reward correctly.

Keep Communicating

Even though your campaign is over, it's important that you stay in communication with your backers via messages, comments, and updates.

If your estimated delivery date is fairly close (within three months of the end of your campaign), you probably won't get too many messages or need to post a lot of updates. If your project takes more than three months to develop and produce the rewards, the more information you can provide your backers before they ask, the better.

If you run into any issues that push out your estimated delivery date, let your backers know via an update. If your project funds, you're expected to send your backers their rewards by when you said you would, so let them know if that isn't going to happen.

Updates are especially important. Whether they can be read by anyone or only backers, they show you're still engaged with the project and the people who gave you their money after you have their money. If you decide to do another Kickstarter project, this current project and how you treat it can be a great endorsement that you've already proven yourself capable of delivering on the promises you make.

Use The Backer Report Spreadsheets

When backers return their surveys, their information is put into backer report spreadsheets you can download from your Backer Report page. You can get to the Backer Report page by clicking on the "View backer report" link in the list of Creator Tools on the left side of the page.

You can use the information in the spreadsheets to print shipping labels and reward checklists. In order to do that, you need to download the spreadsheets, possibly clean up some non-English characters, and create a mail merge template in a word processing program, such as Microsoft Word. A mail merge template lets you define a structure for information once, such as a postal address, and use it as many times as you have information to put in it, like printing out hundreds of address labels.

A Note About Surveys And Backer Report Spreadsheets: If you aren't using the Kickstarter surveys to get information from your backers, the backer report spreadsheets won't be as useful to you (and neither will this chapter of the book) since the spreadsheets won't contain any mailing addresses and the name listed will be the backer's Kickstarter account name, which may or may not be the backer's real name.

Download The Spreadsheets

At the top-right corner of the Backer Report page is an "Export" link. When clicked, an overlay will display with a dropdown list that has each of your pledge levels as options, as well as a "No reward" option as the last entry. The dropdown list will be set to "All reward tiers" by default.

When you click the "Export" button, Kickstarter will compile whatever information it has about each of your backers at that time into a spreadsheet file with a .csv extension.

If you have a lot of backers, or want to come back later, you can click the link "Email me when ready" and you'll get an email from Kickstarter when the spreadsheets are ready to download. The email contains a link, which when clicked, will take you to the Kickstarter website so you can log into your account and see a page with a link to download your files.

If you chose a single pledge level, the file that downloads

will be the spreadsheet file with the .csv extension. You can open it in any spreadsheet program such as Excel or Numbers, or even a text editor, if you don't mind each piece of information being separated by a comma.

If you select the "All reward tiers" option from the drop-down list on the Export overlay, the file that exports for you to download will be a Zip archive file with the extension .zip. When you click on that file, it'll display a folder, inside of which are .csv files for each of your pledge levels.

The file name for each .csv includes the pledge level, the date (month and day) and the time of day when you created the export, as in "Kickstarter Backer Report - $3.00 USD reward - Jan 16 09am.cvs." This is very useful so you know when the files were created and what backer information they contain if you download multiple exports.

You can download your backer report spreadsheets as often as you want. Kickstarter will always provide the information it has as of the time you click the "Export" link. This means as backers return their surveys, addresses are put into the spreadsheets so previous copies you've downloaded are now incomplete.

It's important to understand that any changes you make to the spreadsheets after you download them, such as altering the sort order or replacing foreign characters, will only affect those specific files on your computer. If you download a new set of spreadsheets, your changes won't be in those new files.

Clean Up Non-English Characters

Whatever software Kickstarter uses to save the information from the surveys and put it into the backer report spreadsheets, it doesn't handle non-English characters well. The accented letters used in Spanish, French, and German, and the letters that just don't exist in English that do exist in languages like Polish and Danish, don't translate into useful information. This means you could end up with some oddness in your spreadsheets depending how some of your backers spell their names or where they live.

For example, the German city of "Munich" shows up in the spreadsheet as "M√ºnchen."

So it's in your and your backers' best interest to clean up those odd characters so the reward packages have a chance of getting where they're supposed to go.

Here's a list of the odd characters I've run into and what they should be:

√•	–	å	√©	–	é	√∏	–	ø
√∂	–	ö	√®	–	é	√≥	–	ó
√ñ	–	Ö	≈Ç	–	el	√ò		Ø
√§	–	ä	ł	–	el	√§	–	ä
√Ñ	–	Ä	≈ª	–	Ż	√£	–	ã
√Ö	–	Å	≈ö	–	Ś	√±	–	ñ
√º	–	ü	ƒô	–	ę			
√°	–	á	√ú	–	ü			
√ü	–	ß	√±	–	ñ			

The best way to assure you take care of every instance of an odd character is to do a search-and-replace in your backer report spreadsheets. I also have the odd character list on the Resources page of the *Kickstarter Companion* website so you can copy them off that webpage if you wish (http://www.kscompanion.com/resources).

If you come across an odd character that's not in the list, you can find the correct character by using the Backer Report page and following these steps:

1. Find an instance of an odd character you want to get rid of in your spreadsheet.
2. Now find some part of the backer's name that doesn't include the odd character (EX: "Tom" in "Tom√°s"). Make sure you're referencing the "Backer Name" (second column in the spreadsheet) and not the "Name" since that information came from the survey and isn't searchable on the Kickstarter website.
3. Go to your Backer Report page and do a search. If you end up with more than one result, click on each row and review the Backer Details overlay until you find the correct person.
4. The Backer Details overlay will display the correct character instead of the odd character. You can then copy that correct character off the webpage and use it in your search-and-replace (EX: "Tom√°s" becomes "Tomás").

Depending on your backers, you may have a lot or only a few of these odd characters show up in your spreadsheets.

If you sort the spreadsheet by Country, it'll be easier to check for odd characters since backers from the same country (using the same language with non-English characters) will be next to each other.

And remember, as soon as you make a change to a spreadsheet, that spreadsheet will be different from what you download from the Kickstarter website.

Unfortunately, there's currently no way to correct the odd characters on the Kickstarter website so they're correct in every export, so be sure to keep the files you work on safe and backed up somewhere other than your computer, just in case.

Create A Mail Merge Document

If you have a lot of packages to ship to a lot of backers, you may want to print the shipping labels instead of writing each of them out by hand. Printed labels also have the advantage of being easier to read and with less chance of error as you're using the address as typed in by the backers themselves.

Depending on the shipping service and the software you use, you may be able to print your shipping labels directly from the spreadsheets. In that case, skip ahead to creating checklists.

If you don't have a way to print address labels directly from your spreadsheets, you can create a mail merge template in a word processor program. The mail merge template will take the address information out of the spreadsheet, format it into the correct lines, and make the information ready to print out onto shipping labels that can be bought at office supply stores in various sizes.

For my Wish Cranes project, when I originally thought I'd have around 30-50 backers, I intended to hand-address each envelope. When the campaign closed and I had over 270 backers, I figured out how to create a mail merge template in Microsoft Word.

Depending which word processor program and which operating system you use, the instructions on how to create a mail merge template will be different. You can search online for the specific instructions you need. If you're using Microsoft Word and Excel 2008 on a Mac, you can follow the instructions I've put on the *Kickstarter Companion* website on the Resources page (http://www.kscompanion.com/resources).

Create Checklists

Depending on the complexity of your pledge levels and whether or not you had any add-on/a la carte items, you may want to create a new spreadsheet or text document as a checklist to make sure your backers receive the correct rewards. Your backer report spreadsheets don't have any information about the specific rewards associated with a pledge level, just address information and backer survey answers.

Checklists are exceptionally helpful when it comes to packing rewards, especially when working with a group of people. Using a checklist ensures everyone knows exactly what needs to go in each package and to which backer that package will be shipped.

You can use the same techniques you learned to create a mail merge document to create a checklist that has the backer addresses and their survey answers.

Whether you create a new spreadsheet or text document or just print off your backer report spreadsheets, have some way to keep track of what gets packed and shipped. This reference will be invaluable if there's a problem later on with one of the packages.

Ship The Rewards

With all of your rewards completed and your shipping labels and return labels and checklists printed, you're ready to package and ship the rewards to your backers.

Here are a few recommendations:

- It's better to spend a bit of time putting together secure packages than to have to send new rewards to replace broken ones.
- Ship to international backers first as their packages will have the longest travel time.
- If you have a lot of packages, understand you may be at the shipping facility for a while and plan accordingly. Don't try and squeeze your trip in on your lunch break or show up fifteen minutes before the place closes.

Once you've shipped a backer's reward, you can go to your Backer Report page on the Kickstarter website and select the "Rewards sent?" checkbox for that specific backer. Those checkboxes are for your eyes only; your backers don't get a notification if you use them.

What If Your Project Doesn't Fund?

Not a happy thought, but it's possible your Kickstarter project may not fund. If that's the case, this is what will happen next:

- Per Kickstarter's fixed-funding financial model, no money will be taken from anyone who pledged.
- Your project will still be listed on the Kickstarter website and linked to from your Profile page as a project you created.
- You can still post updates and message backers.

If you want, you can launch a new Kickstarter project. The new project can be the same as the original (although you should probably change something since it didn't fund), or use parts of the first project in a different way. I've seen both done successfully.

You could also take your project to a different crowdfunding website. There are a lot out there, so Google around, ask friends/networks, and maybe there's a better way to raise the money you need than Kickstarter.

Whatever you decide, post an update thanking your backers for their efforts to help you. You can also ask them to sign up for an email list to keep in touch. Since they showed enough interest to become a backer, they likely want to know what you do next.

In Conclusion

It takes a lot of courage, work, time, and attention to create a successful Kickstarter project—more than you probably thought. I hope you found something helpful to you and your project in this book, and that it answered questions you didn't know you had.

You can get in touch with me by using the contact forms on my personal website (http://www.heidi2524.com) or on the website for the *Kickstarter Companion* (http://www.ks-companion.com). I'd love to hear from you with any thoughts you have on my book or experiences you've had creating your own Kickstarter project.

Best wishes,

Heidi Berthiaume

Kickstarter Companion Backers

The following people pledged to my *Kickstarter Companion* Kickstarter project which ran from February 28-March 31, 2014. The project was a success, including the funding of three stretch goals (http://www.kickstarter.com/projects/heidi2524/the-kickstarter-companion-book).

Thank you all, so very much.

Adam Tannir
Adrian J. Mayer
Alan Abair
Alex Barker
Amy Sisson
AmyJalapeño!
Andrew Zimmerman
Angela N. Hunt/Hunt Press
Anonymous
Anthony "Naz" Iannazzi
aois21 publishing, LLC
arvin pilit
Avatars of Alderguard
Beginner's Mind
Ben Dover
Benjamin T Adams
Bernadette Giroux
BibleProphecySchool.com
Bill P
Bob Ash
Brad Rudacille
Brandy Lynn Maslowski
Brenda Lane
Brysen Bristow
Cape Rock LLC
Cara Weston
Carmen
Carolyn E. Cooper
Chad Nimmo
Chris Lin
Chris Lowe
Chris Todd Miller
Christian Lamprecht
Christina M. Parker
Christopher Kimble
Cindi Cox
Cindy Dunn

Colette Black
Connie Taylor
Connor Cochran
Cristal Givens
Daniel Ing
Dave Skaggs
David Brake
Debbie Waller
Denise Gary
Denise Lee
Devin Pearson
Diane Severson Mori
Diann T. Read
Dimitri Frost
Doctor Popular
Don Hodge
Ed and Anne Neufeld
Elizabeth D. Nelson
Elizabeth Hogan
Evan W.
Frank M
Gerry Cardinal III
Gideon R K Murray
Gilly Collinson
Greg Vose
Gwen Reyes
Heidi A. Wilde
Hemal Gala (INDIA)
Holly Heisey
J.T. Entzminger
J.T. Turner
Jala Prendes
James A. Owen
James Donovan
Janix Moon
Jason Safford
Jeff and Marina Benson
Jeff La Belle
Jeff Sanders
Jeffrey J. Warnock
Jennifer Tesolin
Jenniferann LeBlanc
Jeremy Stephen Anderson
John Eric Ladd
John Frewin
John Kelley
Joshua Essoe
K. Byun
Karen Smirmaul
Karl Jahn
Katherine Johnson
Kathryn Henderson
Kathy Dwulit
Kazia Hodges
Kenneth Colley
Kevin Guyer
Kevin J. Anderson,
WordFire Press
Kirk & Laura Bender
Kristin Luna
Lauri Dahl
Laurie A. May
Loa Ledbetter
Loretta Howard
Lucy P
Ma and Pa
Magloft.com
Manolis Sfinarolakis &
Jessica Sun
Marion F. Carpenter Jr.
Mark
Marko CyberCity
Radosevic
Marlena Harris
Melanie Egbert
Melanie Fletcher

Michael C.Dougherty
Michael Gilbert
Michael J. Sullivan
Michael Mendheim
Mignon Fogarty
Mike Scigliano
Mike Ulman
Miles Galliford
Moses Siregar III
Nancy DiMauro Greene
Natalie Strawbridge
Nathan Barra
Nifer Kilakila
Nik Willmore
Noah 'bibulb' Ramon
Origen Clothing Company
Pamela Almoustine Magee Bradford
Patrick Sullivan
Paul Sudlow
Peter McDonald
Philip Som
Rachel Richter
Rae
Richard Kayatt
Rob Hatcher
Robert wiener
Ron Searcy
Ronnie McCord
Roon
Rosemary Clement
Ross Travis
Roxanne Conrad
Roxanne Kenison
Russell Walks
Ruth Sanderson
Sam Shafie
Seriina Covarrubias
Shauna
Shelly Webster
Siobhan McNally
Slade Eide-Ettaro
Steve Blood
Strider Jones
Sue W
Suzanne Gochenouer
Swinka
Tami B
Tanya Hales
Terri Kempton
the hansons
The Ink Knight
Thomas S Darragh
Thylacine
Timothy Kersten
Tom Prats
Tommy Taylor
Tracy and Lisa Mangum
Vanessa Indelicato
Varelie
Velma McKenzie-Orr
Vickie Smith
Victoria Morris
Vincent Villafranca
W. Ryan Ziegler
Wanderer
Wendy Jo Hanninen
White Forest Art
Whitney J Wadlow
Whitney Moses
Zuzka Bachy

Index

D

E

F

G

H

I

J

K

L

R

S

T

U

V

W

Y

12798510R00127

Made in the USA
San Bernardino, CA
28 June 2014